WH

THE RICH
DON'T
DIE BROKE

WHY THE RICH DON'T DIE BROKE

The Financial Prodigy's Secret of the Wealthy

2nd Edition

S. PAUL HORSLEY

ISBN: 978-1720902454

CreateSpace Independent Publishing Platform

Dedication

To my Lord and Savior Jesus Christ. Thank you!
Without Him, we would not have the opportunity
to impact others' lives. www.FaithinGrace.com.

To my wife, Michelle, the love of my life,
and the person who has stood by me and inspired me
since the day we first met.

To our children, Ariel, Ana, and Jack—you are the world
to us, and I am thankful for the privilege of being
your dad and having the opportunity to radically
change your financial life.

To David Pietsch for exposing me to the
Infinite Banking Concept—Thank you.

To every hardworking American who has been lulled
into complacency in a banking, retirement, and estate-
planning system that is set up against you!
May you never again be at the whim of
the existing financial system.

> Contents <

> Acknowledgements <

I want to thank my wife for her steadfastness in my life. Her unwavering encouragement to write and complete this book was instrumental in getting it into its final form. I'm thankful for her positive critiquing, ultimately helping me to craft this book into an easy-to-read and user-friendly financial manual. She is amazing!

Also, without the incredible effort by Renee Garrick, the best editor on the planet (The Grammar Queen), this work certainly would not have appeared in an acceptable form. She was always there helping to guide me through the challenges of writing clearly, always checking and rechecking after every rewrite. The amount of effort on her part is greatly appreciated, and I will be forever grateful.

Finally, I want to recognize my mentor R. Nelson Nash and the relentless dedication he had in the pursuit of furthering the Infinite Banking Concept. He was the true harbinger of what can only be described as the greatest financial tool known to man. His first book, *Becoming Your Own Banker: Unlock the Infinite Banking Concept*, set off a chain of events impacting many lives. Next to him, I thank his beautiful and ever-faithful wife Mary. She steadfastly stood by his side as his perfect helpmate. I will always be honored to have been able to call them my friends.

> Representations and Disclaimers <

Status: The author of this book warrants and represents that he is not a "broker" or to be deemed as a "broker-dealer," as such terms are defined in the Securities Act of 1933, as amended, or an "insurance company," or "bank."

Legal, Tax, Accounting, or Investment Advice: The author is not rendering legal, tax, accounting, or investment advice. All exhibits in this book are solely for illustration purposes, but under no circumstances shall the reader construe these as the rendering of legal, tax, accounting, or investment advice.

Disclaimer and Limitation of Liability: The author hereby disclaims any and all warranties, express or implied, including merchantability or fitness for a particular purpose and makes no representation, guarantee of accuracy, completeness, or warranty of certainty that any particular result will be achieved. Use of all information comes at your own risk. You, the reader, assume all responsibility for risk of loss or knowledge of information contained herein.

The information and illustrations contained herein are assumptions based on examples for demonstration purposes only and should not be viewed for a specific or general outcome for any particular individual or party. Actual individual results will vary based on a wide range of factors and variations unique to each person's situation and circumstance.

In no event will the author, his employees, associated persons, or agents be liable to the reader of this book, or its agents for any causes of action of any kind whether or not the reader has been advised of the possibility of such damage.

> Foreword <

I've had the pleasure of knowing Paul Horsley for several years now and am very pleased at how well he has grasped the deeper meaning of what the Infinite Banking Concept is all about.

The concept of banking is a necessary function in our lives today in order for people to enjoy our standard of living. But the entire financial world is in an awful mess at this time simply because the banking function has been commandeered by the "top-down thinking" of central bankers.

Individuals can insulate themselves from this financial slavery by understanding and adopting the Infinite Banking Concept. Paul has articulated this message well with this book and is a superior practitioner of its message.

R. Nelson Nash

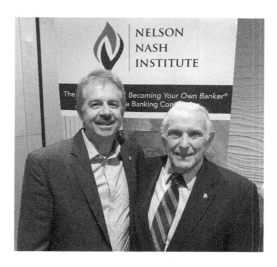

Author S. Paul Horsley and R. Nelson Nash at an
Infinite Banking Concept Think Tank

R. Nelson Nash is known as the discoverer and developer of The Infinite Banking Concept™ and the author of *Becoming Your Own Banker: Unlock the Infinite Banking Concept*. Nash was inducted as a Hall of Fame Member by Equitable. He's also a Chartered Life Underwriter and a Life Member of the Million Dollar Round Table.

> Preface <

In writing this book, I gave thoughtful consideration to share with you what only the rich have known for a long time. Speaking with numerous people, I began to recognize that there are many who wish they knew a better way to use their money, to make wise spending choices, and even how best to store their money while having easy access to it. I wrote this book to make the case that our financial savings and investment system is strongly biased against most people who use it—and to reveal how you can avoid the system's pitfalls, ending up on top and in control of your own money.

You can turn the system around to your advantage, learning from the financial maneuvers used by investment bankers and major corporations in their executive compensation plans—and by politicians in their personal estates. The banking industry has made a cumulative investment of more than $400 billion into the alternative investment strategies unveiled in this book for their own executive retirement and compensation packages—instead of, and in addition to the financial system they push everyone else to use.

You're about to begin a financial transformation. This book is a trustworthy guide for your financial journey, which will change the trajectory of your family's financial life for generations. Let me share a few pieces of my own transformation.

I was trained as a pilot and worked for a major commercial airline. This company filed bankruptcy and underwent a huge merger with a competing airline. At that time, my wife—also a pilot—was employed by the same airline. The merger was a jolting eye-opener for my family, as both breadwinners took a big hit, sending us into financial turmoil.

Shortly after the airline filed for bankruptcy, it alerted the pilot group that our company pensions would be significantly reduced, frozen, and stopped for all future pilots. The company would move what little money remained in the pilots' pension plan into a federal oversight agency called the Pension Benefit Guaranty Corporation (PBGC). That's when the real lesson on money began for our family—the lesson about who actually has our best financial interest at heart.

After the airlines merged, pilots were left with the PBGC and the company 401(k) retirement plan, both government controlled. Frequently in these situations, including our case, employees' monies are allowed to be allocated to other debts, leaving a fraction of their original pension payments, or even eliminating payments entirely. Our professional labor force lost hundreds of millions of retirement dollars. For those long-established in their careers, this magnitude of financial loss is extremely challenging. And later in life, it can prove impossible to recoup. The primary lesson I learned from this event is that when others control my money, I don't.

The 401(k) (referring to a section of the Internal Revenue Code that allows employer-sponsored, tax-deferred retirement savings), the Individual Retirement Account (IRA, also tax-deferred), and every other retirement plan served up by the government or stock market firms push the average person into risk and loss of control. When the political wind shifts, so do government financial policies—and Wall Street gains and losses. These constant changes can cloud the picture of how easy it is to lose your money.

This book will share an inside look at modern financial industries and alternative investment strategies, steering you toward a system that truly favors you and your family. You'll see clearly how to avoid what the rest of the world is doing. Specifically, you'll learn how to pilot your money, with little to no risk, using a simple, effective financial vehicle.

With the government and the Wall Street casino at the wheel, there's only one guarantee—Mr. and Mrs. Average take 100 percent of the risk with a high probability of losing. There's a better way. The wealthy have it figured out—and shortly, so will you.

> Introduction <

Why the Rich Don't Die Broke: The Financial Prodigy's Secret of the Wealthy will guide you through the mystifying world of the financial system in the United States. This book will show you how to overcome the risky monetary system and succeed through the Infinite Banking Concept (IBC).

The Infinite Banking Concept was developed by R. Nelson Nash, author, nationally recognized life insurance agent, and the leader of the Nelson Nash Institute. The institute trains individuals how to utilize this alternative financial strategy and bolster their prosperity.

In short, the Infinite Banking Concept utilizes a Specially Designed Life Insurance Contract (SDLIC), not only for the death benefit, but more importantly, to utilize your own money to finance your life's many financial needs—and without having to dip into your 401(k) or IRA, or use other people's money such as bank loans.

Basically, you'll learn how to become your own banker, developing a simple system of self banking and personal family finance. As a bonus, this system can develop a substantial financial legacy for your family, yet simultaneously allow you to use your money today. Regardless of a person's age or financial situation, almost anyone can benefit.

As an Authorized Infinite Banking Practitioner, I've been personally mentored by the founders of the IBC. As a result, I began teaching individuals the best strategies and techniques for successful IBC implementation and its long-term successful outcome. This book is the culmination of many years of study, sharing what my associates and I have learned together. It breaks down our convoluted US financial system and teaches the Infinite Banking Concept in simple-to-understand terms. As a result, the reader should quickly benefit by gaining an accelerated understanding of the IBC. Throughout the following pages—and as you incorporate the concept—you'll learn several key ideas.

- Use your current household monies to begin enjoying the use of uninterrupted compounding of principal, interest, and dividends 24/7/365 for your entire life.
- Form a yield curve that never inverts, that stays positive and ever growing for life.
- Reuse your money over and over, never losing any of the internal compounding of principal, interest, or dividends.
- Shield your money from risk and loss in the stock market and other financial institutions.
- Shield your money from taxation on your gains.
- Predict growth for your money.
- Begin to capture all current and future interest you pay on debts from all sources.
- Gain 100 percent access to your money with no hidden fees or penalties.
- Overcome inflation and deflation.
- Legally pass money on to your heirs tax free.
- Create a multi-generational financial fortress while using your own money in an ongoing, as-needed basis.
- Rely on a system with a track record dating back more than 200 years.
- Create a rock-solid financial foundation from which everything else grows.

While you may not be aware of it, whole life insurance has a proven track record dating back more than 200 years. In fact, records indicate that in 1759, the Presbyterian Synod of Philadelphia sponsored the first life insurance corporation in America for the benefit of Presbyterian ministers and their families.

I can personally attest to the benefits of using the IBC system. Once you put it in place, you may use your money for anything you choose—and enjoy one of the most secure systems for your money. You can learn the financial strategies employed by politicians, high-end bankers, executives, and the affluent—using the same monies as you do today, just thinking differently regarding how to save for the future and finance your life.

Based on the trusted mentoring that I received from Mr. Nash, there is concern that this country has growing financial strain and is in need of some kind of correction. I'm hopeful the IBC system will be seen as the financial tool of choice and will be utilized by more of the working class.

The destructive recession of 2008 was only a minor speed bump for people who control their money using the IBC. They never lost a cent. Their money kept on compounding, uninterrupted, 24/7/365 inside the IBC system.

I often wonder how the financial leadership gets away with so many blunders and misstatements. Here are a few comments by those who have overseen our banking and financial system over the last 100 years. Note what each one said, and then what really happened afterwards. Is it any wonder that our system is so convoluted? Either they really didn't see the downturns coming, or they just flat out lied. Both are scary answers.

On June 27, 2017, Janet L. Yellen, Chair of the Board of Governors of the US Federal Reserve stated that she did not believe there would be another financial crisis for at least as long as she lives, thanks largely to reforms of the banking system since the 2007–09 crash.[1]

That sounds a bit like the late Irving Fisher, noted Yale economist, who said, just nine days before the 1929 crash, "Stock prices have reached what looks like a permanently high plateau."[2]

Then from Ben Bernanke, who chaired the Federal

Reserve from February 2006 to January 2014, we received these inspirations:

November 21, 2002: "The US government has a technology, called a printing press (or today, its electronic equivalent), that allows it to produce as many US dollars as it wishes at no cost."[3]

November 15, 2005: "With respect to their safety, derivatives, for the most part, are traded among very sophisticated financial institutions and individuals who have considerable incentive to understand them and to use them properly."[4]

March 28, 2007: "At this juncture, however, the impact on the broader economy and financial markets of the problems in the subprime market seems likely to be contained. In particular, mortgages to prime borrowers and fixed-rate mortgages to all classes of borrowers continue to perform well, with low rates of delinquency."[5] (Watch the 2015 Oscar-winning movie *The Big Short*.)

January 10, 2008: "The Federal Reserve is not currently forecasting a recession."[6]

Of course, this was declared as we were heading into the biggest financial collapse of our lifetime . . . so far. Here we are over 10 years later. Will our personal money airplane lose one or more of its engines in flight—or fly safely through blue skies until it arrives at its final destination? It depends on our own financial intelligence in the cockpit.

One of my favorite quotes is by Winston Churchill: "The longer you can look back, the farther you can look forward."[7] It's a great quote that can be applied to piloting—and finance too.

> Introduction <

[1] *Fed's Yellen Expects No New Financial Crisis in 'Our Lifetimes'*, Reuters, accessed April 24, 2018, https://www.reuters.com/article/us-usa-fed-yellen/feds-yellen-expects-no-new-financial-crisis-in-our-lifetimes-idUSKBN19I2I5.

[2] *Stock Market Crash of 1929*, Federal Reserve History, accessed April 24, 2018, https://www.federalreservehistory.org/essays/stock_market_crash_of_1929.

[3] *30 Bernanke Quotes That Are So Absurd You Won't Know Whether To Laugh Or Cry*, Michael Snyder, Business Insider Australia, accessed April 24, 2018, https://www.businessinsider.com.au/bernanke-quotes-2010-12#nov-15-2005-6.

[4] Ibid.

[5] *The Economic Outlook*, Chairman Ben S. Bernanke, Board of Govenors of the Federal Reserve System, accessed April 24, 2018, https://www.federalreserve.gov/newsevents/testimony/bernanke20070328a.htm.

[6] *Bernanke: Feds Ready to Cut Interest Rates Again*, Associated Press, NBCNews.com, accessed April 24, 2018, http://www.nbcnews.com/id/22592939/ns/business-stocks_and_economy/t/bernanke-fed-ready-cut-interest-rates-again/#.Wt93-Jq-pQJ.

[7] IZQuotes, accessed April 24, 2018, https://izquotes.com/quote/37249.

Chapter 1

> The Lies <

This is a story about a lie told for so long that it sounds like the truth. This is how we, the American people, have been led down a destructive financial path from the moment we began to earn our money. The lies within our banking and retirement systems mislead and derail us.

A prominent Wall Street banker made this exact concern known. "Never in the field of monetary policy was so much gained by so few at the expense of so many,"[1] said Michael Hartnett, Chief Investment Strategist for Bank of America Merrill Lynch, on November 1, 2015. In other words, the big gains that the Wall Street bankers have made have been shouldered by the many (us), as we take all the risk with our money in their system.

Have you ever felt suspicious about where you're saving or investing your money? Does earning less than 1 percent interest on the savings accounts or CDs make you wonder if there's something better to do with your money? Do you have concerns about the stock market? For example, the market experts say there's a long-term average return of 12 percent, but you haven't seen that result. How can this discrepancy be explained? If you're like most people, you don't understand what the financial professionals claim. One side says the economy is on fire, but the other warns of eminent collapse; and all those experts are vying for your attention with their "expert analysis." Certainly you can find someone supporting any position at any given time.

Maybe you're like me, who had a portion of every paycheck withheld for a 401(k). Sometimes the quarterly statements showed my 401(k) funds were increasing, but by less than the quarterly deposits I had placed into the account! I was participating in the only way I knew at the time, and my account was managed by the "professionals." I was definitely skeptical and frustrated, not able to overcome the lingering feeling that I'd never get ahead. Ever feel that way?

More than likely, you have a personal checking and savings account, an IRA, and a 401(k). You may also have other investments like real estate or a business, yet you never seem to get ahead either. Most people give little thought as to how our financial banking system works. Unfortunately, it's not set up for you to be the winner.

Who told you about money, or the best way to accumulate money? Was it a parent, or a friend you trusted? How about an employer, accountant, attorney, banker . . . or no one? The funny (or I should say not so funny) thing is that it seems no one is taught in school how money works—or how to manage money. We're just told by "the system" what we should do with our money.

We've been brainwashed to believe we need those long-established Wall Street financial institutions. As sure as death and taxes, we've become complacent, believing that it's absolutely normal to give up hundreds of thousands of dollars—or more—to these institutions over a lifetime. But you don't need those institutions. They need you!

We are the proverbial sheep—uneducated about the bias in the system—who are led to the financial slaughter. The system says, "Do it this way," and—almost to the man (and woman)—most of us step in line and do what the *others* are doing. With that approach, we end up with what everyone else gets: a shot at the Wall Street casino.

Think about it. We assume 100 percent of the risk, they always get paid, and we never know what the financial picture will look like from one year to the next. Who likes that idea? Everyone, it seems . . . because that's what everyone seems to be doing! Instead, wouldn't you love to have a level of risk of almost 0 percent, in an alternative system that could give you almost a 100 percent chance of success, instead of being in the risky financial casino? Keep reading; through the information in this book, you'll have that chance!

Our Story

A number of years ago, my wife and I had growing concerns—not only about our retirement monies, but also in our ability to get ahead financially. We began studying the world of economy and finance, finding it complex and complicated. Ultimately, we stumbled upon the Infinite Banking Concept (IBC). It rocked our world, and it will rock yours if you use a little common sense—which includes reading this book.

Like you, we prefer a place to keep our money safe, growing, and available. People work hard, and yet almost everyone hands their hard-earned money over to banks, brokers, and investment companies without really understanding the consequences and ramifications of doing so. We do it because the system makes it easy to do. We don't understand the investment system, but instead rely on "professionals" who promise we will earn a return on money that we rather blindly pass along to their care. Most people I talk with never participate in the decision of where their money is invested; they leave it to "the pro."

Finance Growth Killers

People would be shocked to know about the obstacles that have been set up along the path as they try to grow their money—and how much they could and do lose in the process. Consider these excerpts from Tony Robbins' book, *Money: Master the Game, 7 Simple Steps to Financial Freedom.*

"If you're getting an 8% gross return on your mutual fund, you're paying as much as 3% in fees on average—let's call it 2%, conservatively. So now your 8% nets you 6% after fees. But we're not done yet. If you're a high-income earner from

California or New York with a 50% federal and state ordinary income tax, you're left with closer to 3% on your investment after all those fees and taxes . . . if you invest with a solid 3% return, it will take you 24 years to double your money."[2]

But the Wall Street casino never gives consistent returns year in and year out, do they?

Not only will the vast majority (96 percent) of actively managed mutual funds *not* beat the market, the professionals charge us exorbitant fees, extracting up to two-thirds of our potential nest egg in fees.[3]

Many people are excited about the "tax-deferred" treatment for a 401(k); but for most employees, the tax cost has been swapped out with "plan administrative" fees. These are charged in addition to the fees paid to the underlying mutual funds, and, according to the Government Accountability Office (GAO), the average plan administrator charges 1.13 percent per year![4] (The GAO is an independent, nonpartisan agency that works for the US Congress. It is the "congressional watchdog," and it investigates how the federal government spends our taxpayer dollars.)

If you own a mutual fund in a taxable account, the average tax cost is between 1.0 percent and 1.2 percent annually, according to Morningstar, an independent investment research firm.[5]

In addition, Tony states that average Americans pay more than half of their income to an assortment of taxes: income tax, property tax, sales tax, tax at the pump . . . you get the picture? (According to what many experts estimate, currently, that's 54.25 cents per dollar.)[6]

Beyond that, about one-third of the left over money will pay down interest charges on houses, cars, student debt, and more. That leaves you with just 28 percent of your money to pay for everything else—including your savings.[7]

Then there's the inflation factor and the loss of *the time value of money*, which will be discussed in detail in Chapter 7.

Suspicious for Good Reason

You are about to learn that *average rates of return* mean nothing to your personal results in stock market investments. Unfortunately, there is excessive use of the phrase *average rates of return* in stock market jargon. These analyses are used to convince you that investing in the stock market should produce growth. Those with investments that have lost value have been convinced to "hold" their investments because—over the long term—they should increase in value.

One view of rates of return comes from Dave Ramsey, a best-selling author who focuses on financial advice. This is an excerpt from his blog post at daveramsey.com, *Return on Investment; the 12% Reality.*

> When Dave says you can expect to make a 12% return on your investments, he's using a real number that's based on the historical average annual return of the S&P 500.
>
> The S&P 500 gauges the performance of the stocks of the 500 largest, most stable companies in the New York Stock Exchange—it's often considered the most accurate measure of the stock market as a whole.
>
> The current average annual return from 1923 (the year of the S&P's inception) through 2016 is 12.25%.[8]

Ramsey's website says this is the most accurate measure of the stock market. Most financial professionals and banks, which earn income on your investments, agree that it is a reliable guidepost. Actually, investment gain or loss doesn't result from average rates of return. Our results are generated by the compound annual growth rate. Consider this explanation from moneychimp.com in their article entitled "Compound Annual Growth Rate (Annualized Return)."

> A problem with talking about average investment returns is that there is real ambiguity about what people mean by "average." For example, if you had an

investment that went up 100% one year and then came down 50% the next, you certainly wouldn't say that you had an average return of 25% = (100% - 50%)/2, because your principal is back where it started; your real annualized gain is zero.

In this example, the 25% is the simple average, or "arithmetic mean." The zero percent that you really got is the "geometric mean," also called the "annualized return," or the CAGR for Compound Annual Growth Rate.

Volatile investments are frequently stated in terms of the simple average, rather than the CAGR that you actually get. (Bad news: the CAGR is smaller.)[9]

Authors Glen Zacher and Jayson Lowe, in their book *The Bankers' Secret*, share the following:

Mutual fund companies and stockbrokers are quick to display impressive charts of historical average rates of return, and because of these comforting numbers, people go through their lives with a false sense of security. Unfortunately, this practice is only perpetuating one of the biggest investment myths of all time. The false belief is that in the ups and downs of your investment's returns, the average rates of return will always be in your favor.

This is one of the most popular gimmicks used within the financial industry. To demonstrate, we are going to examine the hypothetical life of a $100,000 investment over a four-year period. Let's say you can get an average rate of return of 25% from one of the top mutual funds. This could be any number, but the point is to see that an average rate of return does NOT mean your money actually grows by that alleged average. Here is our hypothetical example:

Year 1: 100%
Year 2: -50%
Year 3: 100%
Year 4: -50% divided by 4 years =
                    25% average rate of return

A 25% return seems pretty impressive, right? But wait a minute, let's forget about the percentages on paper and look at the corresponding dollar amounts year by year:

Start of Year 1	Invested Money	$100,000
End of Year 1	100% growth	$200,000
End of Year 2	50% loss	$100,000
End of Year 3	100% growth	$200,000
End of Year 4	50% loss	$100,000

It's not a 25% increase is it? It is a gain of 0%![10]

Diversified Asset Allocation

This term is used by most, if not all, financial planners. *Diversified asset allocation* is one of their most heavily used phrases. This phrase should raise questions, but most people mistakenly assume a sense of comfort and safety. The system of diversification within the stock market has bothered me since I was exposed to it years ago. They use this term because they don't know where to invest a client's money in order for it to work safely (risk free) for them. *Diversified asset allocation* traditionally refers to spreading a portfolio of money into different stocks, mutual funds, bonds, metals (gold, silver, and the like) and other commodities, each with varying degrees of risk. Risk is what we are trying to minimize. Uninterrupted compounding of money is what we want.

In general, by doing what everyone else is doing, you'll get the results that everyone else is getting. This is a valuable lesson that we should always have at the top of our minds. But most people don't think that way.

Diversification is also an overused term. People diversify because they are unsure of the risk of loss, and they know there's assumed risk of loss when investing in the stock market. A Certified Financial Planner (CFP®) is paid to offer investment advice, typically directing investments and moving people's money around over time into different investment tools like stocks, bonds, and mutual funds. When the stock market is or appears to be rising, CFPs typically move your money there. When it's not rising, they typically move your money into something less volatile, say another stock, mutual fund, bond, or commodity—but rarely into a cash position unless things are really bad, or when you direct them to do so. Many times they just leave the money (investment) alone to ride the mystifying ups and downs of the stock market, hoping that it rises more than it falls.

Fact: Every time they move your money, they get paid. The value of that payment is lost to you forever because their payments come out of your funds either yearly or every time they move your money around. That's ongoing lost compounding—forever!

Depending on your level of wealth, that loss can climb into hundreds of thousands of dollars over your lifetime. Let me be clear, I'm not a Certified Financial Planner. In addition, I am referring to the Certified Financial Planner in general terms, not specifically targeting anyone or any particular business. I'm simply trying to clarify how the system works.

Here is another example illustrating the effect of the loss of compounding. Consider this: one penny. If the penny doubled in value every day for a month, what would it be worth? It would be worth an amazing $5,368,709.12. Now that's compounding! But let's say on any given day in that month you took the value of that day and used it. The very next day there would be *no value* (no pennies compounding). You would have to start all over. If you had waited one more day, you would have been able to use the entire amount from the previous day and still had a considerable amount from which to continue compounding . . . but it would still be less compounding overall.

You might decide to take something less than the full value on a given day to use it. The effect on the compounding would be the same: greatly diminished long-term compounded gains. This example is extreme, yes; but the idea is to convey to you the significance of having anything less than the whole amount compounding for you as you go forward. When money is removed from the system, it's no longer able to compound. In the Infinite Banking Concept system, that same money never ever stops compounding 24/7/365 . . . for life. **This is key**, and it will be explained more fully as you continue to read.

My wife uses an analogy to further the point. Imagine that you are sitting in a commercial jet airplane. While preparing for takeoff, you see fuel leaking out of the wing and all over the ground. How long would it take you to say something to stop the plane from taking off? My guess is, not long. You would surely want the problem fixed before takeoff, otherwise you would never make it to your destination. Upon completing this book, you will understand the significance of the information; and you could look at your money and the leaking gas tank the same way, with IBC being the fix.

Mainstream Misguidance

Who created this system of rules and finance? They're the very people who demand you take all the risk, while they control all the money for as long as possible. These are people who make up our federal government, Wall Street banks, other financial institutions, and major corporations. As long as you have your money in their system, there will be loss of control and risk of losing your money. Many people don't understand this system—and don't realize there's an alternative.

I believe the mainstream financial system is an inefficient, top-down bureaucratic system that has failed us. If it's so good, why do they highly regulate it and try to create new ways to direct our money with new investment ideas?! Big money institutions and the government, hand-in-hand, work with our money, charging fees and taxes while we take 100 percent of the risk. They make it so easy for us to use their system that it seems as if theirs is the only one available for holding our money, saving, and investing, which prevents people from considering that an alternative self-banking system could possibly exist.

Consider the Glass-Steagall legislation (the Banking Act of 1933). It was installed to keep commercial banks and investment banks separate from each other to prevent collusion. Over the years, it has slowly been dismantled and repealed by politicians, who were pushed to do so by those who control the money. Today there is a movement to bring it back, which would be a good thing.

Those who are invested in the current financial system hold onto it as if their lives depended on it. In reality, their lives depend on letting it go. It's time for a financial revolution.

Of course, financial revolution means a new approach, thinking differently.

Steve Jobs was a true visionary. The creator of Apple, he could see differently from most, envisioning cutting-edge technology that would change the way the world interacted. Job's vision was, essentially, "I will create what you would have really wanted if you only knew it was possible."[11] With this book, I'm attempting to illuminate your understanding of the current financial system and the alternative system that could give you what you have always wanted but didn't think possible. If you're like most people, this has everything you've wanted but didn't know was available. You won't be alone when that recognition happens for you.

The great Albert Einstein once said, "Compound interest is the eighth wonder of the world. He who understands it, earns it . . . he who doesn't . . . pays it."[12]

[1] Danielle DiMartino Booth, *Fed Up*, (New York, Penguin Random House, 2017), 1.

[2] Tony Robbins, *Money: Master the Game, 7 Simple Steps to Financial Freedom*, (New York: Simon & Schuster, 2014), 278.

[3] Robbins, 110.

[4] Robbins, 114.

[5] Robbins

[6] Robbins, 274.

[7] Robbins, 275.

[8] "Return on Investment; the 12% Reality," Dave Ramsey, accessed April 2, 2018, https://www.daveramsey.com/blog/the-12-reality.

[9] "Compound Annual Growth Rate (Annualized Return)," Moneychimp, accessed April 3, 2018, http://www.moneychimp.com/features/market_cagr.htm.

[10] Glen P. Zacher, CFP and Jayson C. Lowe, *The Bankers' Secret: A Simple Guide to Creating Personal Wealth for Canadians* (Edmonton, AB Canada: McGuire Financial Inc., 2014), 43–44.

[11] Harry S. Dent Jr. and Andrew Pancholi, *Zero Hour: Turn the Greatest Political and Financial Upheaval in Modern History to Your Advantage* (New York: Portfolio/Penguin, 2017) 120.

[12] "10 Reasons why Compounding Interest is the 8th Wonder of the World," Andrew Sather, accessed June 19, 2018, https://einvestingforbeginners.com/compounding-interest/.

Chapter 2

The Solution

I get it. Everyone's working hard all day, returning home to run the household, just to repeat the process over and over again. There's little time to be the jack-of-all-trades in our daily lives, which is why we use the easiest system for our day-to-day banking and savings.

I also appreciate that everyone is naturally skeptical about a "new system" until they see other people profiting from it. Since the Infinite Banking Concept is an idea most people have never heard of, it is important to explore why it's worth learning.

The average workers don't realize that "the system" is working against them. I didn't realize it until my friend David told me about a system he had learned from his wealthy friends. That's when the day finally dawned on my financial life. By the end of this book, the light of day will arrive for you and your money, too.

As my wife and I arrived at David's home for our initial conversation, we looked at each other and wondered what we would learn from him. But we knew he was a successful, wealthy businessman. As we sat down in his house, never in a million years would I have guessed what we'd be discussing.

David started the conversation by asking us a few simple questions. "Do you use a bank? How about insurance? Do you use insurance for your cars, your house?"

"Of course," we said.

"How about your savings, like an IRA, 401(k), savings account, or real estate? Do you have those kinds of things too?" he continued.

"Well, yes," I said. "We have all of those. Why do you ask?"

He just looked at us for a minute, then said, "Well, who told you about those kinds of things, and how did you come about picking each of them? How much time and effort did you spend vetting each one?"

For the life of me, I couldn't figure out where he was going with his line of questions. He proceeded to ask how much trust we had in each of our savings and investment choices. He had captured my attention; a puzzling thought arose. *Trust?* I realized then, I had believed the system was set up to work for me. It was supposed to take care of me.

Then he wanted to know when we first heard about IRAs and 401(k)s. We told him it was probably back when we got our first jobs, several decades ago. Those companies made it easy to just sign up for them and have the money taken directly out of our paychecks and put into these accounts. Simple.

"Is that a good idea?" he asked.

"Well, it makes it easy," I said.

"Yes," he said, "it is easy, isn't it?"

Knowing the caliber of who was talking, I sensed that he was leading us down an important road. Again, I wondered what he meant. *What is it that he's trying to tell us?*

David followed up by asking us the question that changed everything. "What are the two biggest expenses most people have in life?"

We thought for a minute. *Hmmm . . .*

Then my wife said, "Interest."

And I said, "Taxes."

"Correct!" he said. "What if you could begin to capture your current outgoing interest payments and all the interest you will pay in the future? Would you ever have a need to invest in any other investment vehicle?"

"I'm not sure," I said, trying to do the math in my head.

"Think about it for a minute," said David. "How much does the average homeowner spend on home or other real estate mortgage interest? Hundreds of thousands of dollars over a lifetime. People are attracted to low rates of interest when buying homes, not giving the volume of interest a thought.

"Do you know the difference and why it's so important? Here's a hint: The banks get paid up front so it takes you much longer to pay off that huge debt . . . and they can make even more interest. The joke about refinancing at a lower rate of interest is just that—a joke. The banking system loves it because the banking system continues to get the biggest chunk of the monthly payment in the early years. Get it? It's not set up for you to be the winner. Further, what about all the other interest paid out—for example cars, credit cards, student loans, every large purchase we make?!"

The thought was intriguing. *Could it really be possible to start capturing our own debt's interest?*

So, back to the IRA and 401(k). David asked, "Why do you think an IRA and 401(k) are good ways to save?"

We looked at each other and I said, "First of all, I can defer taxes to a time later in life. That's good, right? Well, at least that's the way I've been looking at it for my entire working life."

He just looked at us, raised his eyebrows and asked, "What will your tax rate be at the point of your retirement? Additionally, what income tax bracket will you be in?"

I piped up and said, "It'll be lower because I'll be making less money." That's one of the selling points the professionals share when they encourage their clients to use an IRA or 401(k).

He just looked at me, his face blank.

My thoughts raced. *Whaaaat? Did I miss something?*

Then, he asked the most significant question.

David leaned forward and asked, "Do you really want to have a lower standard of living—by having less income than in your working years? You'll still have living expenses, perhaps you'll want to travel more, and presuming medical expenses will be rising at that time . . . do you want to have less income?!"

Boom. That question stopped me cold. It hit me hard. No one had ever proposed this to me before.

"No," I muttered sheepishly.

David continued. "Actually, you have no idea what tax rates will look like, or the income tax bracket you'll be in, either. So no one can be confident they'll be paying less taxes in the future, right?"

"No," I said. I was beginning to feel a little uncomfortable by this point.

My wife and I were both thinking the same thing. *What else could we have missed?*

"Let's think about farming," said David. "If you were a farmer who plants seeds, like a corn seed—one kernel, for example. That one seed of corn produces one corn stalk containing two ears of corn containing about 1,400 corn kernels, or seeds. My question to you is, would it be better for the farmer to pay a tax on the one original seed . . . or the 1,400 harvested seeds?"

That seemed simple enough. "The one seed," I said.

"Right!" he answered. "But, think about this. When you're paying taxes on your IRA and 401(k) monies, you're paying on the harvest!"

"Wow!" That was a defining moment, to say the least.

David proceeded to ask, "Who's overseeing or managing your money once it's locked into the IRA or 401(k) for 10, 20, 30 years or more? And who's taking all the risk . . . I mean *all* the risk? And who is *guaranteed* to make money on your money?"

Shockingly, it was at that moment I realized we—and the rest of America—have been duped! My wife and I were taking 100 percent of the risk, and had no guarantees. With these plans, we—along with everyone else—might not make one cent, or we may lose it all, not even maintaining our original capital investment! I liken it to casino gambling. It's a legal form of gambling with the money I had planned on using in my later years!

The fact is that we have access to only a very small fraction of our money at any given time. We're constrained by multiple government rules. And any money we may need is allowed only as a loan with very regimented specifics. Without a doubt, this is a lockbox without a key, and no access to our own money, which we might need to use.

I also knew that if we withdrew any money before 59½ years of age, we'd pay an additional 10 percent tax just to have the ability of using our *own* money! This whole IRA and 401(k) idea was really beginning to stink. All of my IRA and 401(k) money has been locked up in the bureaucratic system all these years. I've had to borrow money from another part of the system for my house, cars, and college education . . . just to make their system work! The government, Wall Street, and the banks lock up our savings and make us use their money to finance the rest of our lives. Amazing!

While this was sinking in, David continued, "Is a dollar more valuable today or tomorrow?" And before we had a chance to answer, he explained, "If you understand our governmental system of printing unsecured money, then you see one dollar today is more valuable than one dollar tomorrow. Based on the math of inflation, you begin to understand how the financial retirement system is working against you."

"What's the alternative, David?" I asked.

He paused, looked at us, and knew we were feeling like some of the most gullible people alive. He smiled gently and went on, "There's hope. There is a way, a much better way to use your money."

My wife and I looked at each other with relief, smiled, and quickly dialed in to the next phase of our financial education.

"How much research did you put into the bank you use today?" asked David. "You know, the one with your checking and savings accounts?"

My wife responded quickly, "It's the bank our employer uses for direct deposit." That would mean no research at all.

It was handpicked by someone else! And we'd never given it any thought at all.

David then asked, "What kind of research did you do on your insurance company, you know, the one you use for your cars, house, and your lives?"

Research? The only research I had done was price comparisons and, maybe, name recognition.

Continuing on, he said, "Okay. Now, if you were going to invest your hard-earned money—you know, like in an IRA, a 401(k), in the stock market, or really in any other kind of investment—what kind of a rate of return would you consider satisfactory?"

I hesitated. What kind of return would I like, or what am I getting? "Seven percent!" I blurted.

David said, "Okay, now we have a baseline from which we can work."

Alright, I thought. *He's going to show me how to make seven percent interest on my money!*

"What if there was a way to pay off your outstanding debt," asked David, "and also capture all the future interest you would pay to someone else, and best of all, avoid paying taxes on the money you made inside your new investment vehicle? What if that could happen?"

My mind spun. *You're crazy!* Instead I asked, "How is that even possible?"

He smiled. "There is a way! And this idea has been around for over 200 years. What do you think about that?"

"Seriously—200 years?!" I said. "And I haven't heard about it? We're all ears."

"What if I told you this is the same process that many of the exceptionally wealthy have used—and are currently using—to build their families' financial empires?" asked David.

"Like who?" I asked.

He started listing one name after another, people I recognized. Names like Buffet, Rothschild, Walt Disney, JC

Penney, countless others. Most major banks around the world, most major corporations, and—don't be shocked—your Washington politicians! But we *were* shocked. What was this idea . . . and how did it work?

"Have you ever heard of life insurance?" asked David.

"Sure," I said.

"What do you know about it?" he asked.

"Well, I know that we should buy enough term life insurance and invest the rest of our money somewhere, like in the stock market, for example." I sounded like a bad sound bite.

"Invest in an IRA or 401(k)?" He queried with a smile. Then he asked that thought-provoking question again, "Who told you that? Was it the same people who told you the IRA and 401(k) were good ideas?"

Again, feeling as if we had been duped by years of poor financial advice, I began to recognize there was so much more to learn.

David continued, "You use a bank today, right? You put your money into it, and take your money out of it, right?"

"Yes, sir, that's how it works," I replied, all smiles.

"What if you could create your own banking system, a system that worked very similarly to your current bank, but with much, much better benefits to you?" he asked. "You could make deposits and withdrawals from the system similarly to the bank you use today. In addition, you would be able to earn dividends and interest on your money 24/7/365. In fact, you would never stop making money on your money for as long as you live. Sound good so far?"

"Yep, keep talking."

David asked, "When you write a check today, or use your debit card, and use it to pay for something—anything—can you ever use that money again . . . or is it just gone?"

"Well, of course it's gone. I used it," I retorted.

Then, in another defining moment, he presented something I could not envision at first. "What if you used the

43

system I'm about to describe to you, and you could simply deposit your hard-earned money into your own system, emulating the good qualities of how a bank works. In addition, this new banking system of yours would also make it possible to use your money *over and over and over again*, and never stop earning money on your money, compounding day in and day out, making dividends and interest—at the same time you're using it for purchases until the day you die?"

"Sounds incredible, if it's real!"

"It is!"

I asked him what the system was called.

"It's the Infinite Banking Concept," he said, "and it's encompassed inside a Specially Designed Life Insurance Contract (SDLIC) through a dividend-paying, mutually owned whole life insurance company."

I didn't know what to say. I surely couldn't repeat what he had just said, and I had been studying world finance for years. "So, tell me more," I said.

David knew we had just shifted financial gears, and he was trying to make a big impression so he threw out another thought. "Let's say you are retired and withdrawing from your 401(k) or IRA or savings account. That money is forever decreasing and, once spent, is of no further value, right?"

"Correct."

"What if, in the Infinite Banking Concept, these same dollars you were using, which normally would be decreasing in value, were actually increasing in value—daily?"

I was at a loss for words, but wanted to know how that could be.

David began telling us how he was introduced to this idea, how he had begun his own banking system, and how he had captured his debt and the interest he had previously been paying. The person who introduced David to this system was a student of R. Nelson Nash.

Since my enlightening conversation with David, he and

I have been on a quest to spread the word about this unique system and its similarities to banking. Some years ago, I had the honor to meet Mr. Nash. He became one of our greatest friends and a personal mentor.

Since the first edition of this book, my friend and mentor R. Nelson Nash has gone home to be with the Lord. I spoke with him just days before he "graduated from this earth" as he would have said. He was in good spirits, knowing his days here were drawing to a close. It was a call I will not forget. My wife and I miss him terribly, right along with every person who knew him.

Nelson was a most amazing man in so many ways. He always had time to talk, to share something new he had just discovered, and to give that big Nelson smile. Truly, one of my most treasured memories of him was when he would share the following with those he was teaching: "This concept is not complicated, it is just different from the way the majority thinks and behaves. You have to think long range. You can't be afraid to capitalize. Be an honest banker with yourself. Don't do business with banks except for a checking account if at all possible; rather use your IBC policy." And most recently he would constantly say, "Rethink your thinking. If you have an open mind, you will discover a whole new financial world."

We will be forever thankful to Nelson. He changed our family's financial future for generations.

We look forward to seeing him again.

Chapter 3

Understanding How Our Money System Works

Before we can dive into the nuts and bolts of how Infinite Banking works, I thought it best that we spend just a short time understanding how money actually works—and further, how banks work and how the financials of insurance companies operate. Without this context, it will be difficult to put all the moving parts together and garner a solid understanding. Bear with me; while you may fully understand the next paragraph, please keep in mind it represents the cornerstone for the rest of the book.

Let's get your mind in sync with the very basic concept of how a bank works. It's a pretty simple concept. A bank has two basic types of accounts, checking and savings. Typically, we deposit money into either or both of these accounts and withdraw money as needed. The checking account is for everyday use, while the savings account is a way to store your money for some future event. As long as the money is in the bank, it has some financial value. When your money is removed from the bank (for whatever reason), you have no more money in the bank. There is no more value in the bank account.

Should you need a loan (a car loan, for example), the bank is there to accommodate you if you qualify for the terms of the requested loan. When the loan is taken, it typically does not directly affect your checking or savings accounts, meaning that your accounts were not used to create the loaned money. The loan is created from a different source of money within the banking system.

The bank charges a rate of interest over the term of the loan. You would repay the debt with interest as prescribed in the terms of the loan agreement from the bank. There is typically no flexibility on the repayment schedule once it's established. When the loan is fully repaid, the bank has received the return of its principal loaned money and the interest that was charged; and you have the product you bought.

Next, let's look in greater detail at our system of money and how it works. I feel certain you'll experience a paradigm shift that leaves you thinking, *I never saw that coming*. Check this out . . . I know you've heard this or some version of it: The federal government must raise funds through taxation or borrowing in order to create money to spend. In other words, government spending is limited by its ability to tax or borrow. If you're like most people, there's no surprise in hearing that statement, correct? People say it all the time. You have no alarm bells going off in your head. Surely, that statement has been heard for a long time, so it must be true, right? Wrong! That statement is a big fat lie! Who said it—and where did it come from? A wise friend told me years ago, if you tell a lie long enough, it will become the perceived truth. That's exactly what has happened.

Here's a fact: Any government needs to charge its citizens taxes to force the use of their specific currency. Take a moment to consider this—citizens are charged a tax, which is payable only in the specific currency of that government. If that were not the case, any two or more people could simply barter and exchange products or services, never producing a medium of exchange or currency. In the United States, the general understanding of our tax system has obscured actual need. Taxes charged by the federal government are not required in order for our government to have money to spend. Year after year the federal government operates with a tremendous deficit. The word *deficit* elicits great authority. Our country has a deficit because, from day one, it never started with any money of its own. It had to create money, and from that first day the money creation has been called *deficit money* or *deficit spending*. If our government didn't create this money, from what source would we get the US dollar? This system of creating currency and spending can succeed as long as the country has natural resources, commodities to produce and export, and a population that uses it for a means of financial exchange.

Here's another fact: The federal government spending spree is in no case constrained by revenues, meaning there is no solvency risk. In other words, the federal government can always make any and all payments in its own currency, no matter how large the deficit is, or how small an amount of taxes it collects. How? The US dollar isn't monetarily tied to any item or any commodity—gold, for example. Therefore, it doesn't have a limiting factor within its exchange. It has no real value that can be measured. We measure its value based on the price of goods and services daily, such as fuel at the gas pump or food at the grocery store. The US currency has value because people trust that the federal government will honor its exchange. As a society, we've used US currency since 1861.[1] Typically, we don't question its value. Our government, however, is dependent on having citizens use its currency. If our country's citizens didn't use their currency and thereby give it inherent value, the government would have no spending power. Because our currency is no longer backed by gold, we term it "fiat money," which we'll discuss in greater detail later in the book. Actually, the entire world's monetary system is based on fiat money. Suffice it to say that there's no money in the world system that's currently backed by anything other than the government that creates it.

Again, we'll discuss this more later, but for now let's consider how our banking (money) system really works. This is beyond the two basic bank accounts from above and the created deficit money just described. Again, you must understand this will be additional, newly created money that is above and beyond the deficit money from the last paragraph. From an aviation perspective, we are changing planes to get to our ultimate destination. We're leaving the deficit-money plane and embarking on the fractional-reserve-banking money plane.

Let's say you deposit a dollar in your bank. How much of that dollar could the bank lend to someone else looking for a loan? You might say 25¢, 50¢, or anything up to the whole dollar, right? That's what most people believe. But the real answer is that banks can lend out *multiples* of that very dollar.

Put another way, banks can lend out more money than they have on hand in deposits. A $1 deposit could turn into $10, $20, or more for the bank. This banking system is called fractional reserve banking. Ever heard of it? It's been around for decades; it's just rarely discussed—and even less understood. Equate this statement as an analogy to the Infinite Banking Concept—never heard of it.

Let's take it another step. The Federal Reserve, also known as the Fed, is a central banking system created by the federal government back in 1913 to try to steer the economy away from downturns. The Fed is the entity (actually a private company) that creates the US government deficit money as described above. Under the direction of our executive branch (the President) and then the legislative branch (Congress) after great debate, the US dollar is currently produced by the Federal Reserve. The money is then disbursed into the US banking system.

Once a dollar is deposited into a bank, that bank can lend out multiples of it, albeit within limits set by the Federal Reserve. The bank has a cap on the number of derivatives of the dollar that can be created. (Don't know what a derivative is? In finance, it's a contract that derives its value from the performance of an underlying entity. In this case, the US dollar is the basis for the creation of multiples of that same US dollar.) The system is based on the mandates of the Federal Reserve, which fluctuate depending on the Fed's money policies at any given time. (Interestingly, the Federal Reserve has authority to mandate aspects of our monetary system not directly overseen by the US government—interest rates, for example.)

When those newly created dollars are loaned and then deposited into other banks, what happens? All those dollars can then be loaned out in multiples all over again. Yes, over and over again. Do you see the potential dangers of this cycle? Where does the bank get multiples of dollars to lend out? The answer is . . . out of thin air. Seriously. The bank creates the money by simply changing its accounting ledgers. Banks do not and are not required to have an equal number of dollars in house as the dollars they are lending out. There are efforts behind the scenes to keep this knowledge limited. Shocked? I was too. The knowledge is out there, you just have to dig for it; but first you need to know it even exists. The same holds true with IBC.

How is this possible one might ask? I've included a link to a valuable book about this very topic. In his book, *The 7 Deadly Innocent Frauds of Economic Policy*, Warren Mosler details the practices of banks and tax policies. Download your free copy at http://bit.ly/1viv5vg. Mosler is an economist, hedge fund founder, engineer, inventor, and founder of Mosler Automotive. His book is an easy read—certainly educational and entertaining.

As we continue discussing bank deposits, we should know that deposits in banks are insured by the Federal Deposit Insurance Corporation (FDIC). The FDIC's purpose is to provide stability to the economy and failing banks. It guarantees (insures) a specific amount of financial deposits for its member banks.

What most people don't know is that all deposits are limited. The FDIC insures deposits according to their categories of ownership and how the accounts are titled. The standard limit on deposit-insurance coverage is $250,000 per depositor, per FDIC-insured bank, per ownership category. If your account's balance is larger than that, and the bank defaults, you'll lose the money over the $250,000 limit in that bank. To top it off, the FDIC isn't required to return your entire lost deposit to you immediately; but thankfully, they typically return the insured portion within a few days. Following is an excerpt from the FDIC titled "5 Common Misconceptions About FDIC Insurance . . . and the Real Facts." I encourage you to read the rest of the webpage article too; it's eye opening.

MISCONCEPTION 1: FDIC insurance coverage is based on the type of deposit you have. For example, a checking account is insured separately from a certificate of deposit (CD).

The Facts: FDIC insurance coverage is based on how much money each depositor has in one of several "ownership categories" at each bank—single accounts, joint accounts, revocable trusts, certain retirement accounts and so on—not on the deposit product itself.

Let's assume that Jane Smith has both a CD and a checking account at one bank. Both accounts are in Jane Smith's name alone, and she hasn't named beneficiaries to receive the funds upon her death. The two accounts are considered single accounts for ownership purposes, and they are added together in calculating the deposit insurance coverage; the fact that they are different types of bank products does not provide separate deposit insurance coverage. In this situation, Jane's two accounts would be added together if the bank failed; and $250,000 would be insured.

MISCONCEPTION 2: Adding beneficiaries to Individual Retirement Accounts (traditional and

Roth) and certain other retirement accounts can increase the FDIC insurance coverage.

The Facts: The FDIC adds together all the retirement accounts that a person has at a bank in the insurance category called "Certain Retirement Accounts" and insures them up to $250,000, regardless of the number of beneficiaries designated to receive the retirement accounts upon the owner's death. That insurance category also includes accounts such as Simplified Employee Pension (SEP) IRAs and self-directed 401(k) and Keogh plan accounts. *Self-directed* means the consumer chooses how and where the money is deposited.[2]

So many unknowns. Again, risk is a common theme, and we (not the banks) are taking 100 percent of it.

Before the US dollar was removed from the Gold Standard, there was an equivalent measurement of gold owned by the government for each dollar bill printed. That means for every dollar created, there was an exact amount of gold owned by the US Government. There could be only so many dollars in circulation based on how much gold the government owned.

Since 1973, the US dollar has not been tied to any type of government-owned commodity like gold or other precious metal. That means banks don't need deposits from outside sources (you and me) to create money, because our money isn't linked to an equivalent commodity to keep it stable, such as described previously. Before 1973, the value of our currency was based on existing amounts of actual mined gold. Banks paid higher interest rates for a savings account versus a checking account because higher interest paid on deposits assisted them in attracting more deposit money. Having deposits provided the dollars needed to create loans and make more money in interest charged.

Today, banks can create money, not by printing it, but by adjusting their ledger balances, in order to make a loan on paper to a customer. A bank essentially doesn't need to pay interest to their customers' account deposits, because their need for capital deposits has changed so significantly. Again, this is because the bank doesn't need our dollars to fund their loans. But we need bank loans (conventional loans and credit cards) for big-ticket items like houses, vehicles, and anything we can't pay cash to buy. First the bank creates money out of thin air and lends it out to earn interest from us. That's predominantly how the bank earns its profits—interest.

The need for financing in our lives is of utmost importance when you consider how much of it you really do. Consider the amount of money you pay out each month, year, and over your life in interest and fees. Would the ability to control that process be financially beneficial both now and in the future? Start thinking in generational terms and the picture begins to get bigger and clearer.

As you keep reading, you'll learn how to eliminate the bank—the middleman—and pay yourself the interest on your purchases!

To illustrate how the bank earns money from your activity, take the example of getting a loan for a new car. You go to your bank, they offer you their best terms, and you agree. The bank credits your account with the loan amount by creating a simple deposit in the ledger. (They type numbers into your account and . . . poof! There it is.) Then the dealer gets the money and you get the car. Further, the bank collects your monthly payments for principal and interest on the loan. Separately, the car dealer deposits your payment (bank loan) amount into their bank, and the whole system starts again. Money has been added to the entire system like magic.

Again, bankers can lend more money than they have in deposits; the amounts are limited by the Federal Reserve, which regulates that derivative multiple based on how the economy is doing. Further, think of derivatives as the accelerator and brakes of your car. The Federal Reserve uses derivatives to speed up or slow down the economy. The federal government uses taxes to do the same thing. That should keep your head spinning for a while. You can have further clarity on derivatives and taxes by reading Mosler's book referenced previously.

How Insurance Company Money Works

Let's consider how insurance companies operate financially. Unlike banks, which have fewer requirements for balancing their loans with their deposits as it relates to fractional reserve banking, the insurance industry is under a different set of rules—rules that one would expect to be applied to the banking industry. For example, for every dollar an insurance company lends, they have to hold a dollar in their reserves. That's a far cry from fractional reserve banking.

A life insurance company is governed by state laws within each state for which it holds a license. In addition, every state has its own sponsored Guaranteed Insurance Fund (GIF). You can look at this as insurance for the insurance companies' beneficiaries. A percentage of the revenue from a life insurance company's earnings is required to be deposited in the company's state sponsored GIF. This is a pool of money from all licensed insurance companies in each state, held in the GIF for safekeeping.

Life insurance companies are further rated with a Comdex score. Comdex is a composite index score averaging the ratings given to life insurance companies by major insurance-rating organizations including A.M. Best, Standard & Poor's, Moody's Investors Service, and Fitch Ratings. Think of it as a report card for the insurance companies. It produces a score for each life insurance company, from 0 to 100, showing where it's ranked among all the insurance companies. (Wouldn't it be great if a bank's rating of safety could be viewed in such a way?) If you were to use an insurance company, we strongly recommend that life insurance companies with scores of 95 or better be used. They're incredibly safe institutions for an individual's financial assets as rated by the Comdex ranking. In fact, most banks have investments in life insurance companies because of their financial stability. In the financial world, life insurance companies are known as a Tier 1 financial investment for investment banks, meaning they are among the safest of places to store equity of core capital. According to Investopedia, "Tier 1 capital is essentially the most perfect form of a bank's capital—the money the bank has stored to keep it functioning through all the risky transactions it performs, such as trading, investing and lending."[3]

Life insurance companies must think financially very long term—20, 30, 40, 50, 60, 70 years or more down the road, for understandable reasons. Having said that, their investments are very conservative and forward thinking.

[1]"History of United States Currency," MyCreditUnion.gov, accessed April 24, 2018, https://www.mycreditunion.gov/Pages/money-101 -history-united-states-currency.aspx.

[2] "5 Common Misconceptions About FDIC Insurance . . . and the Real Facts", accessed May 17, 2018, https://www.fdic.gov/consumers /consumer/news/cnfall14/misconceptions.html.

[3] "Tier 1 Capital," Investopedia, accessed April 4, 2018, https://www .investopedia.com/terms/t/tier1capital.asp.

Chapter 4

Types of Life Insurance Contracts

Let's define basic life insurance terminology, which is easy to misunderstand. Further, I'll introduce a special kind of life insurance that may not be familiar to you. We'll explore with great detail the functionality of this type of insurance contract, allowing you to appreciate the ways it can benefit your family and your estate.

First, there are two basic types of life insurance: *term* and *permanent*.

Term life insurance is like renting life insurance. It covers the person insured for a specific period of time, then ends. It does not have a cash value, rather it only pays a monetary benefit if and when death occurs. Should the term life insurance expire before the person's death, there will be no death benefit paid to the estate. In fact, should that same person want to purchase more term life insurance after the original term expires, generally the cost can be prohibitive.

Rather than term insurance, which ends on the agreed-upon date, the alternative is called permanent life insurance. In general, this option continues throughout the life of the individual and may have a cash value, depending on various scenarios. Typically, when the person dies, at any age, the death benefit is paid. Permanent life insurance is offered as *whole life* or *universal life* insurance with various options. Universal life insurance is a variable product with uncertain outcomes based on different moving pieces. As to the focus of this book and IBC, let's make one thing crystal clear: No one should ever use a universal life or variable universal life or its derivative in constructing an IBC policy. The only product recommended by authorized IBC practitioners is the whole life insurance policy underwritten by specific mutually owned, dividend-paying companies. And going forward, that one is the type I will focus on.

Most life insurance companies are owned by their stockholders. But there are a few mutually owned life insurance companies, meaning that the ownership of the company is its policyholders. These policyholders have permanent whole life insurance, the value of which is generated from the uninterrupted compounding of annual premiums, the earned dividends, and the earned interest within each policy. The distinction between stockholders and policyholders is important. Stock-owned companies pay their stockholders the dividends, not their policyholders. Thus, the money invested by stockholders has little effect on the value of each individual policy. Mutually owned companies pay policyholders guaranteed interest on their money in addition to potential dividends. Each year, when the interest and dividends are paid to the policyholder by the mutually owned company, the interest and dividends cannot ever be removed from the value of the policyowner's life insurance contracts.

Dividends are by definition a return of premium. They also typically respond to the Fed's interest rate fluctuations, generally on an annual basis. That means if the interest rate set by the Federal Reserve goes up or down, the dividend scale could—and sometimes does—follow. This is important to remember as we continue our discussion.

Now, I can introduce the specific key that allows you to take advantage of the vast benefits of the IBC system. The powerful tool that's essential to this system is a Specially Designed Life Insurance Contract (SDLIC). This contract insures an accelerated cash value, along with the compounding of your money, uninterrupted for your entire life!

In all other types of whole life insurance policies, your money is subjected to the volatility of interest rates, the Wall Street casino, and other various moving pieces; thus the compounding of the policy can be interrupted, diminished, and even completely eliminated to the unknowing owner! That's risk. With an SDLIC, your chance of losing money is reduced to almost zero.

Chapter 5

Nash's Financial-Noise Canceling System

What is meant by "noise canceling system" is akin to silencing or significantly limiting the current monetary system's risk with our money. The financial noise is deafening. According to R. Nelson Nash, "The only way to quell the noise is to think differently." Nash was referring to his Infinite Banking Concept (IBC), which utilizes a Specially Designed Life Insurance Contract (SDLIC). I believe there's no better place for your money than your own SDLIC.

Nash is the harbinger of this financial revolution. More than 40 years ago this man was praying for a financial solution to the significant financial struggle he was experiencing. His answer came in what has come to be known as the Infinite Banking Concept. The system had been used in varying degrees by many affluent families for decades, but it was never taught to the masses.

One of the goals of this book is to show you how easy it is to set up your financial life using the IBC, which utilizes an SDLIC. You may not know what an SDLIC is, but continue on; you will. It's an investment vehicle in which the IBC is the driver. In piloting terms, the SDLIC is the airplane for the IBC pilot. The pilot uses the airplane to get where he's going. Once you understand it, I'll bet you too will see why the rich don't die broke.

Working with an SDLIC is simple in anyone's financial life. To avoid the fallacy of many different thoughts and objections, let's make a few points very clear. Generally, it matters not your income. It matters not your age. It matters not your health. It only matters that you start using the IBC financial strategies through an SDLIC.

Again, age, health, and income are typically not limiting factors in the ability to create an SDLIC. In other words, almost anyone can create one when under the guidance of an authorized IBC practitioner.

The sooner you start, the sooner the uninterrupted compounding of principal, interest, and dividends begins. When that is fully understood, life will be different. Remember the penny example previously discussed on page 32? This is huge.

Before we dive into some of the nuts and bolts of the IBC Specially Designed Life Insurance Contract, it's worth noting several things. First, there's a specific method behind the development, design, and strategy of a proper SDLIC as it relates to the Infinite Banking Concept. The first intent of this book is to share with you what an example of an SDLIC looks and acts like. To be sure, there are other variations and specific techniques used that are not discussed in this book. While utilizing these unique IBC techniques is of great benefit to the individual, to dive into the explanations of them all is beyond the scope of this introductory book. At its conclusion, however, you'll be able to do several things: One, articulate the basics of the Infinite Banking Concept and an SDLIC; and two, be able to understand and take advantage of the significance of the differences between the traditional financial system and that of the IBC system.

The second intent of this book is to clarify how the two terms *IBC* and *SDLIC* work together. The SDLIC materializes the IBC. Infinite Banking is a concept. It creates an alternative option to finance one's life—outside of the world's banking system. This concept builds wealth, creates a tool to use for self-financing your life's ongoing needs, and allows for the bigger-picture view of your financial estate's goals over both the short term and the long term. It's a different way of thinking about money, banking, and the use of each. IBC includes a strategy that utilizes a properly designed SDLIC and appropriately exploits its attributes as further defined in the following pages. Again, in my flying terminology, the SDLIC is the plane, and the IBC is the pilot. The pilot uses the plane to get to the destination.

The SDLIC could exist outside of the IBC system, but this is very unlikely. There are only several hundred authorized Infinite Banking Concept practitioners (of which I am one) in our country of more than 320 million people. Without the knowledge of the authorized practitioner, there would be little chance of acquiring an SDLIC, because most life insurance agents have no knowledge of them. Further, an agent needs to be aligned with one of the few life insurance companies in existence that can produce an SDLIC. Perhaps again, my flying experience can give a helpful analogy. You wouldn't put a small-aircraft private pilot in the captain's seat of a commercial airliner and expect a successful flight any more than you would go to a typical insurance agent down the street and expect to acquire an SDLIC. You couldn't get to your destination in either case because neither the pilot nor the agent is equipped to handle the matter at hand.

The Mechanics of an SDLIC

Let's begin to unfold a Specially Designed Life Insurance Contract, which, as explained previously, is created and provided by a specific kind of life insurance company. An insurance policy is a contract between the insurance company and the policyowner.

It's important to understand that there are three distinct parties within every life insurance contract, (also known as a life insurance policy): the owner, the insured, and the beneficiary. It is important to understand that the owner of the SDLIC has full control of the SDLIC, meaning the owner makes all the decisions and controls everything about it. Let's look at a few scenarios.

- The owner of the contract is responsible for providing the direction of the contract, for example, paying the premiums, designating the beneficiary, determining the ongoing use of the dividends.
- The insured is the person whose life is covered by the contract upon his or her death.
- The beneficiary of the contract is the person who (or entity that) receives the payment of the death benefit amount specified within the contract.

Any person can be one or two of the parties listed above. However, one person must be designated as two of the three contract parties. Here are examples:

- You own the SDLIC, and it is insuring your life. The beneficiary is one or more persons, businesses, or organizations. A beneficiary does not have to be related to you.
- You own the SDLIC, it is insuring a relative or a person of interest in your business, and you are the beneficiary.
- A relative or business partner owns an SDLIC that insures your life and said relative or business partner is also the beneficiary.

The primary purpose of an SDLIC is to develop one's own personal financial lending and money-compounding system. There are four basic financial parts to every Specially Designed Life Insurance Contract.

- Base Premium
- Paid-Up Additions (PUA) Rider
- Cash Value
- Death Benefit

An insurance policy premium is generally viewed as a payment for insurance. Using an SDLIC, you should think of the premium payment as the equivalent of making a deposit into a traditional bank account. The Base Premium (think bank deposit) has two primary purposes. It creates and builds dividends (if any), and it creates the base death benefit amount over the life of the contract.

The Paid-Up Additions (PUA) rider—again, think bank deposit—also has two purposes. First, the PUA brings an earlier-than-normal available cash value to one's SDLIC. This happens because the PUA monies are additional premium amounts deposited by the owner of the contract, beyond the Base Premium. Having early-available cash value sets the SDLIC apart from most life insurance contracts. In this system, the PUA starts an accelerated process of uninterrupted compounding of interest and dividends for both the Base Premium (deposit) and the PUA Premium (deposit). This increases the contract's cash value and makes it available much sooner than it would be without the additional premium deposits.

Secondly, the PUA buys additional paid-up whole life insurance death benefits (money paid upon the death of the insured). The additional benefits are added to the existing contractual death benefit every time more PUA is deposited into the SDLIC. The PUA is an accelerator of funds through the contract's cash value, and simultaneously increases the death benefit.

Finally, the death benefit is the amount paid to the beneficiary, one or multiple persons or entities, at the time of death of the insured.

To be clear, the ongoing available "cash value" is the monetary amount (determined specifically by the owner, as will be explained later) that can be borrowed against the SDLIC by the contract owner as needed. The cash value is a key component in the SDLIC and the Infinite Banking Concept. Having the ability to use your money to finance your life's needs while capturing the interest that would have been lost

to some other entity is priceless. As you will begin to understand, using other people's money to finance your life results
only in the loss of more money working for you. With the
introduction of the SDLIC, your money begins to work for
you in multiple ways and starts the removal of the outside
lenders used by most people. Put another way, you begin
flying the plane yourself rather than sitting back and letting
someone else pilot the plane.

Let's clarify the details of how this borrowed money works
in regard to the SDLIC. Again, only the policyowner can borrow against the available cash value. To be clear, the owner
collateralizes the available cash value against the defined
death benefit as illustrated below. The insurance company
then issues the collateralized loan to the owner. The actual
loaned money comes from the insurance company, not from
the SDLIC specifically. This can happen as many times over
one's life as needed. The specific insurance companies have set
up a system that makes this process very simple. It's nothing
like borrowing from a bank; in most cases one simply calls the
insurance company or fills out a simple loan request docu-
ment online. In addition, like most institutions, the insurance
company needs to utilize something for collateral. But, in this
case, the insurance company doesn't care what the money is
used for, as it uses the contract's death benefit as the collateral
needed to cover the borrowed money. If a death benefit is
claimed while a loan is outstanding, the insurance company
will pay the contractual death benefit amount, minus the collateralized loan amount at the time of death. In a sense, the
policyowner is self-insured. In other words, policyowners are
ensured their estates will not have the burden of outstanding
debts at their deaths. As a sidenote, the policy loans can be
utilized throughout the life of the policy with relative ease.
Typically, the cash value is available about 30 days after the
policy is put in force; and from that point forward, a request
to borrow money can be completed in just a few days. The

only limiting factor is how much cash value is available at any given time. Typically there is no set minimum amount of available cash value that can be collateralized, and you can be collateralized up to all available cash-value monies.

As you will begin to understand, this unique system gives a contract owner the flexibility to grow the money inside the contract and also use the available cash value outside the contract at the same time—in any way you choose. That little sentence is very powerful! Yes, your money can be used more than once *and at the same time* both inside the SDLIC and outside the SDLIC—and never lose the ability to continue making uninterrupted compounding of every cent that's deposited into the system. And just about now the thought of my penny story should be starting to repeat itself.

Nash has always taught that our need to finance (borrow money) is one of the biggest factors of our entire financial lifecycle. Typically, we go to a bank or some other institution to borrow money, and we give interest to that institution for the temporary use of its money. Conversely, being able to use the SDLIC as a banking system is extremely effective and efficient. Collateralizing your available Net Cash Value from an SDLIC is quick and easy, involving little paperwork or red tape, and it grows the contract value even more, as you'll learn. Begin to consider the possibilities with what you've learned thus far. What if your parents had utilized this system and passed along the knowledge, combined with whatever they had developed financially? I believe you begin to see the generational legacy benefits. It gets better; keep reading.

As we dive in, it should be noted that Base Premiums (deposits) and PUAs (deposits) interact perfectly together in a well-designed SDLIC. Unlike the convoluted system of the stock market and the banking sector where success or failure could happen at any moment, producing significant risk, in this system, you're shown what will be provided financially for each year in the future.

Opposite is a one-page example of an SDLIC that we'll study together. Later on, you'll find several other illustrations showing other examples; however, I will not be dissecting those in great detail.

This SDLIC sample represents a 50-year-old male who is a non-smoker. To be clear, this person is starting his SDLIC at age 50. There is no age that is the wrong age to begin an SDLIC. Remember, age is only a starting point for IBC; and IBC is not primarily about insurance, rather it is to be viewed as a financial tool with a kick at the end.

The sample chart illustrates a simulated person's specific financial situation, goals, and objectives within an SDLIC. Practically anyone at any age can start an SDLIC with the guidance from a qualified IBC practitioner. Again, each SDLIC is tailored to the policyholder's specific financial situation.

Let's begin with important terms. Refer back to the sample SDLIC chart opposite; notice the terms *Guaranteed* and *Non-Guaranteed*. In the Guaranteed columns on the left side, the owner is guaranteed the amounts of money listed in annual Contract Premium, Net Cash Value, and Death Benefit.

The Non-Guaranteed columns on the right side include the addition of possible Annual Dividends and interest that would increase the Net Cash Value and Death Benefit. Dividends add to the cash value of a policy and are to be reinvested back into the policy each year. Again, there's no sense in missing out on additional death benefits or the uninterrupted compounding money for life. While dividends are never guaranteed in any SDLIC, the payment of annual dividends is commonplace; and for some mutually owned life insurance companies, dividends have been paid since the inception of the company. In the case of one company we use, they have a 112-year history of operation, including the payment of dividends *every year*! I'll state clearly, past historical practice does not predict future dividends, but it truly is amazing that this company hasn't missed even one year since 1905!

		Guaranteed			Non-Guaranteed Assumptions 100% of Current Dividend Scale					
Age	Year	Contract Premium	Net Cash Value	Death Benefit	Premium Outlay	Surr to Pay Prem	Annual Dividend	Increase in Net Cash Value	Net Cash Value	Death Benefit
51	1	50,000	36,717	883,167	50,000	0	6,904	43,621	43,621	890,071
52	2	50,000	77,875	961,747	50,000	0	7,268	48,656	92,276	988,252
53	3	50,000	119,999	1,037,803	50,000	0	7,666	50,263	142,539	1,084,308
54	4	20,000	133,988	1,037,803	20,000	0	8,812	23,533	166,072	1,105,471
55	5	20,000	148,024	1,037,803	20,000	0	9,057	24,119	190,190	1,128,002
56	6	20,000	162,104	1,037,803	20,000	0	9,321	24,728	214,918	1,150,462
57	7	20,000	176,235	1,037,803	20,000	0	9,598	25,365	240,283	1,172,885
58	8	20,000	190,422	1,037,803	20,000	0	9,869	26,016	266,299	1,195,276
59	9	20,000	204,669	1,037,803	20,000	0	10,142	26,689	292,988	1,217,617
60	10	20,000	218,976	1,037,803	20,000	0	10,439	27,389	320,377	1,239,927
61	11	0	225,423	461,449	0	0	4,010	13,442	333,819	679,142
62	12	0	231,929	461,449	0	0	4,305	13,940	347,759	687,646
63	13	0	238,459	461,449	0	0	4,636	14,426	362,185	696,542
64	14	0	245,016	461,449	0	0	4,983	14,943	377,128	705,860
65	15	0	251,596	461,449	0	0	5,327	15,455	392,583	715,589
66	16	0	258,213	461,449	0	0	5,652	15,978	408,561	725,685
67	17	0	264,881	461,449	0	0	5,943	16,494	425,054	736,077
68	18	0	271,618	461,449	0	0	6,220	17,031	442,086	746,707
69	19	0	278,425	461,449	0	0	6,482	17,560	459,645	757,536
70	20	0	285,291	461,449	0	0	6,772	18,108	477,753	768,569
71	21	0	292,194	461,449	0	0	7,086	18,646	496,400	779,837
72	22	0	299,084	461,449	0	0	7,479	19,183	515,583	791,421
73	23	0	305,913	461,449	0	0	7,931	19,704	535,287	803,412
74	24	0	312,696	461,449	0	0	8,349	20,218	555,505	815,793
75	25	0	319,443	461,449	0	0	8,771	20,756	576,262	828,536
76	26	0	326,148	461,449	0	0	9,182	21,277	597,539	841,617
77	27	0	332,788	461,449	0	0	9,629	21,795	619,334	855,056
78	28	0	339,327	461,449	0	0	10,142	22,311	641,645	868,921
79	29	0	345,709	461,449	0	0	10,741	22,809	664,454	883,312
80	30	0	351,906	461,449	0	0	11,388	23,299	687,753	898,296
81	31	0	357,900	461,449	0	0	12,058	23,773	711,525	913,899
82	32	0	363,677	461,449	0	0	12,715	24,201	735,726	930,102
83	33	0	369,261	461,449	0	0	13,340	24,636	760,362	946,860
84	34	0	374,646	461,449	0	0	13,968	25,057	785,418	964,159
85	35	0	379,805	461,449	0	0	14,588	25,404	810,822	981,983
86	36	0	384,701	461,449	0	0	15,200	25,652	836,475	1,000,320
87	37	0	389,306	461,449	0	0	15,823	25,836	862,311	1,019,175
88	38	0	393,607	461,449	0	0	16,108	25,634	887,945	1,038,215
89	39	0	397,594	461,449	0	0	16,385	25,379	913,325	1,057,377
90	40	0	401,258	461,449	0	0	16,642	25,059	938,383	1,076,651
91	41	0	404,663	461,449	0	0	16,899	24,864	963,247	1,096,047
92	42	0	407,875	461,449	0	0	17,124	24,769	988,016	1,115,542
93	43	0	410,893	461,449	0	0	17,337	24,647	1,012,663	1,135,129
94	44	0	413,712	461,449	0	0	17,525	24,474	1,037,137	1,154,787
95	45	0	416,315	461,449	0	0	17,676	24,200	1,061,338	1,174,485

Short-term and long-term planning is necessary for an SDLIC to work as an Infinite Banking tool. One must start thinking and planning like a banker in terms of deposits, withdrawals, interest, and dividends. Bankers like these terms, and we should too. This is how bankers make profits—and how people using the self-lending Infinite Banking practice can make additional money from their Specially Designed Life Insurance Contracts. Thinking long term—first, developing the ability to finance just about every purchase over one's life . . . and second, passing on the financial legacy—this knowledge is truly one of the greatest gifts a family could give and receive.

Speaking of family legacy, when do you think you will die? No one knows, of course; but let's set the stage for the next piece of knowledge we'll need to transform your financial life using this financial strategy. Typically, when a person buys life insurance, he or she has one consideration in mind: the beneficiary. It's all about taking care of loved ones and handling any financial concerns after one's death. With the SDLIC, that will be the eventual outcome also; however, the owner of this contract is able to use all of the cash value throughout his or her entire life. It can be used in any manner the owner sees fit, all while continuing to compound its growth internally. This is such a rare (and remarkable!) concept that most people miss it. Consider this: Is this concept possible with any other financial or investment tool you know of? Once your money is placed into a retirement account, it's as if that money is locked up in prison. A bank doesn't offer this value for your savings! The coverage, value, and flexibility an SDLIC offers is . . . genius.

Let's more closely examine the sample contract provided above.

First Line, Owner Age 51, Contract Year 1

Age	Year	Contract Premium	Net Cash Value	Death Benefit	Premium Outlay	Surr to Pay Prem	Annual Dividend	Increase in Net Cash Value	Net Cash Value	Death Benefit
51	1	50,000	36,717	883,167	50,000	0	6,904	43,621	43,621	890,071

In the first line, Year 1, consider the contract premium of $50,000 as the equivalent of a $50,000 bank deposit. While the contract is not a bank, it stores your premium deposits, allowing them to compound uninterrupted for your entire life.

Continuing across line Year 1 under Guaranteed amounts, the Net Cash Value and Death Benefit columns represent the cash values for the end of that specific year of the contract. Going down each column in the previous table, you can see what the cash values are in each subsequent year-end of the contract. This is Guaranteed money and it will never be less than what is represented.

Looking to the right side of the page, under Non-Guaranteed Assumptions, note the additional columns showing an Annual Dividend and Increase in Net Cash Value. This represents money from the guaranteed side and adds the projected annual dividends, revealing the projected increases to the contract holder's Net Cash Value and Death Benefit. Each year's dividend is based on the company's dividend rates as set in the current year.

The dividend value can go up or down from year to year, typically based along the Federal Reserve interest rate adjustments. As of this writing, the Federal Reserve had the interest rate set at less than 1 percent. At this minimal rate, if the rate decreased there would be a minimal decline in dividend value. Should the Federal Reserve increase the interest rate, one's contract dividends could increase in value and compound more going forward. With the same rate increase, the numbers in the Non-Guaranteed side of our sample contract may increase *above* the insurance company's projected numbers going forward in time. Amazing!

Following along the Year 1 line, the chart shows that the $50,000 Contract Premium (deposit) leads to a projected Net Cash Value of $43,621 at the end of the year under the Non-Guaranteed figures on the right side of the chart. The $43,621 is about 87 percent of the $50,000 premium. Some may ask, *Why not 100 percent of the premium?* Typically, over the first few years of any insurance product, there is a spread between what is deposited and what is available because the actuaries have determined a certain cost of the insurance and the possible outcomes that could occur. There are also administration fees within the company itself. As noted earlier, the insurance company certainly is taking the risk insuring individuals. However, they have a long-standing history of accurate projections from their internal company actuaries for all projected costs and death benefits. Keep reading, you're going to like the numbers as time progresses.

It should be noted here that it typically takes between 30 and 45 days for the premium deposits to clear the system before one can initially access the available cash value. At other times from that point forward, the available cash value is immediately accessible; and should you as the contract owner want access to it for any purpose—it can typically be in your hands in a week or less. This request for your cash value can be done online in just a few minutes or by phone call to the insurance company directly. Simple.

On the other hand, a contract owner doesn't ever have to utilize any of the available cash value from the SDLIC, but that owner would in effect be losing money by not utilizing (borrowing) money against the contract, as will be explained shortly.

It's not hard to decipher that if the insured person dies in Year 1, the Death Benefit would be $890,071 (in the Non-Guaranteed far right column) and would pay out to the beneficiary that entire sum of money tax free. If the contract owner does *not* borrow the full available cash value, let's say it's the full $43,621 from the initial $50,000 premium deposit, the Death Benefit of $890,071 (to the estate) would have cost the full $50,000.

But *with* the $43,621 loan, the math would look like this:

$50,000	Initial premium deposit
-$43,621	Loan amount
$6,379	Total cost for the resulting death benefit

The borrowed cash value would be subtracted from the death benefit. The $890,071 minus the borrowed $43,621 leaves the actual death benefit total to be $846,450. The policyowner would have deposited only $6,379 for the $846,450 death benefit. This is an incredible exchange on your money, and the insurance company is taking most of the risk—instead of you.

Second Line, Owner Age 52, Contract Year 2

Age	Year	Contract Premium	Net Cash Value	Death Benefit	Premium Outlay	Surr to Pay Prem	Annual Dividend	Increase in Net Cash Value	Net Cash Value	Death Benefit
51	1	50,000	36,717	883,167	50,000	0	6,904	43,621	43,621	890,071
52	2	50,000	77,875	961,747	50,000	0	7,268	48,656	92,276	988,252

Moving across the Year 2 line, you'll see that the Death Benefit is $988,252, which is an increase of $98,181 from Year 1. Note: From this point forward, the discussion will continue to use the Non-Guaranteed columns, as this includes dividends, which the company has consistently paid over the years.

The $98,181 increase from Year 1 to Year 2, subtracted by the Year 2 premium deposit of $50,000 is $48,181. In other words, the contract made a net increase in Death Benefit of $48,181 in Year 2. I don't know about you, but I love free money, and so will my heirs!

Third Line, Owner Age 53, Contract Year 3

Age	Year	Contract Premium	Net Cash Value	Death Benefit	Premium Outlay	Surr to Pay Prem	Annual Dividend	Increase in Net Cash Value	Net Cash Value	Death Benefit
51	1	50,000	36,717	883,167	50,000	0	6,904	43,621	43,621	890,071
52	2	50,000	77,875	961,747	50,000	0	7,268	48,656	92,276	988,252
53	3	50,000	119,999	1,037,803	50,000	0	7,666	50,263	142,539	1,084,308

In this line, note that Year 3 is the final year that the premium deposit is $50,000; it decreases to $20,000 the next year. The Increase in Net Cash Value of $50,263 is more than 100 percent of the $50,000 premium deposit, and it's money available for use by the contract owner. The Death Benefit column increased by $96,056, to $1,084,308. Are you seeing a trend?

Fourth Line, Owner Age 54, Contract Year 4

Age	Year	Contract Premium	Net Cash Value	Death Benefit	Premium Outlay	Surr to Pay Prem	Annual Dividend	Increase in Net Cash Value	Net Cash Value	Death Benefit
51	1	50,000	36,717	883,167	50,000	0	6,904	43,621	43,621	890,071
52	2	50,000	77,875	961,747	50,000	0	7,268	48,656	92,276	988,252
53	3	50,000	119,999	1,037,803	50,000	0	7,666	50,263	142,539	1,084,308
54	4	20,000	133,988	1,037,803	20,000	0	8,812	23,533	166,072	1,105,471

Beginning in Year 4, the deposit has actually decreased to just $20,000 and continues at that lower amount through Year 10, revealing another piece of the "specially designed" (SD) part of the SDLIC.

Fifth Line, Owner Age 55, Contract Year 5

Age	Year	Contract Premium	Net Cash Value	Death Benefit	Premium Outlay	Surr to Pay Prem	Annual Dividend	Increase in Net Cash Value	Net Cash Value	De Ben
51	1	50,000	36,717	883,167	50,000	0	6,904	43,621	43,621	890,0
52	2	50,000	77,875	961,747	50,000	0	7,268	48,656	92,276	988,
53	3	50,000	119,999	1,037,803	50,000	0	7,666	50,263	142,539	1,084,
54	4	20,000	133,988	1,037,803	20,000	0	8,812	23,533	166,072	1,105,
55	5	20,000	148,024	1,037,803	20,000	0	9,057	24,119	190,190	1,128,

Moving down to the Year 5 line, the $20,000 results in a Net Cash Value of $24,119, giving the owner a $4,119 increase over the deposit amount. The Death Benefit continues to rise as well. As can be seen, there are a number of positive things happening that will continue to happen as time moves forward. There is no comparison between an SDLIC and any other financial tool.

Through Year 5, the SDLIC owner deposited a total of $190,000, and $190,190 is the expected Net Cash Value in Year 5, which would be available for use in any increments. Further, the Death Benefit increases to $1,128,002.

Here is an interesting sidenote in Year 5. By deducting the sum of deposits thus far (Years 1–5) from the Death Benefit ($1,128,002 − $190,000), you would see a resultant $938,002 net Death Benefit. It could at this point be considered a no-cost policy . . . because you'd have use of the available cash value. Adding in the annual dividends of Years 1–5, you end up with a projected $190,190 Net Cash Value in Year 5. Yes, it gets much better!

The owner of this contract is looking at a projected Increase in Net Cash Value of $24,119 in Year 5. If you divide the projected Increase in Net Cash Value by the Contract Premium ($24,119 ÷ $20,000), the owner sees a 1.206 percent return on investment (ROI). Let me share that 1.206 percent is an increase of nearly 21 percent. This illustrates my point that the uninterrupted compounding of the principal, interest, and dividends in Years 1–5 is making good progress, to put it mildly. If there was a death in Year 5, the contract would pay out $1,128,002. But let's say that doesn't happen, and let's continue the conversation.

Tenth Line, Owner Age 60, Contract Year 10

Age	Year	Contract Premium	Net Cash Value	Death Benefit	Premium Outlay	Surr to Pay Prem	Annual Dividend	Increase in Net Cash Value	Net Cash Value	Death Benefit
51	1	50,000	36,717	883,167	50,000	0	6,904	43,621	43,621	890,071
52	2	50,000	77,875	961,747	50,000	0	7,268	48,656	92,276	988,252
53	3	50,000	119,999	1,037,803	50,000	0	7,666	50,263	142,539	1,084,308
54	4	20,000	133,988	1,037,803	20,000	0	8,812	23,533	166,072	1,105,471
55	5	20,000	148,024	1,037,803	20,000	0	9,057	24,119	190,190	1,128,002
56	6	20,000	162,104	1,037,803	20,000	0	9,321	24,728	214,918	1,150,462
57	7	20,000	176,235	1,037,803	20,000	0	9,598	25,365	240,283	1,172,885
58	8	20,000	190,422	1,037,803	20,000	0	9,869	26,016	266,299	1,195,276
59	9	20,000	204,669	1,037,803	20,000	0	10,142	26,689	292,988	1,217,617
60	10	20,000	218,976	1,037,803	20,000	0	10,439	27,389	320,377	1,239,927

In Year 10, the specific ROI is 1.369 percent, or about a 37 percent gain based on the sum of all of Years 1–10 gains in interest and dividends. Again, this figure comes from dividing the Increase in Net Cash Value of $27,389 by the $20,000 premium. If we add up Years 1–10, we get a total Net Cash Value of $320,377. The total premium deposits to date equal $290,000. Doing the math, $320,377 divided by $290,000 gets you an overall (Years 1–10) ROI of 1.104 or 10 percent, and a $1.2 million death benefit, and the use of all the available cash value.

Eleventh Line, Owner Age 61, Contract Year 11

Age	Year	Contract Premium	Net Cash Value	Death Benefit	Premium Outlay	Surr to Pay Prem	Annual Dividend	Increase in Net Cash Value	Net Cash Value	Death Benefit
51	1	50,000	36,717	883,167	50,000	0	6,904	43,621	43,621	890,071
52	2	50,000	77,875	961,747	50,000	0	7,268	48,656	92,276	988,252
53	3	50,000	119,999	1,037,803	50,000	0	7,666	50,263	142,539	1,084,308
54	4	20,000	133,988	1,037,803	20,000	0	8,812	23,533	166,072	1,105,471
55	5	20,000	148,024	1,037,803	20,000	0	9,057	24,119	190,190	1,128,002
56	6	20,000	162,104	1,037,803	20,000	0	9,321	24,728	214,918	1,150,462
57	7	20,000	176,235	1,037,803	20,000	0	9,598	25,365	240,283	1,172,885
58	8	20,000	190,422	1,037,803	20,000	0	9,869	26,016	266,299	1,195,276
59	9	20,000	204,669	1,037,803	20,000	0	10,142	26,689	292,988	1,217,617
60	10	20,000	218,976	1,037,803	20,000	0	10,439	27,389	320,377	1,239,927
61	11	0	225,423	461,449	0	0	4,010	13,442	333,819	679,142

In Year 11 the Contract Premium drops to zero, which reduces the Death Benefit on the far right side to $679,142; remember that the Base Premium (deposit) dictates the

Death Benefit. However, from here the projected Increase in Net Cash Value and the Death Benefit continue to grow unabated until the day the owner dies—at an ever increasing rate. Year 11 increases by $13,442 without any further deposit (Contract Premium). Remember, this illustration does not reflect how an SDLIC might be designed for you; rather it is an attempt to illustrate the mechanics of a sample SDLIC. There are variations in every SDLIC, and each owner will dictate the desired end results.

Overall, this SDLIC is becoming more efficient in growth and value. As a pilot, I compare the progression of the SDLIC to flying an airplane. Like a pilot during takeoff using full engine power, SDLIC owners start their banking contracts with the Base and PUA deposits.

While the plane is cruising with less power, it's traveling faster than it did during the takeoff and climbing phase, and it needs less power to keep up a constant speed. Similarly, the SDLIC keeps increasing in value while you have the ability to adjust the amount of deposits after Year 1.

The airplane at level flight and the SDLIC after the few years of deposits . . . each becomes a more efficient vehicle as it moves forward in time. There may even be a time when the total deposits in one's first SDLIC exceed the amount that can be held within the SDLIC. In this case the additional monies can be directed into another SDLIC to start the process over again. This isn't necessarily about creating one SDLIC, but multiple SDLICs that can change the entire family's financial structure and legacy.

Here is another example of an SDLIC. This time the illustration reflects a 19-year-old male. It looks different from the previous illustration, and it shows another way to construct the SDLIC. Notice the Contract Premium deposits stay consistent throughout the years. As described previously, the $10,000 Contract Premium (deposit) is made up of the Base and the PUA. In this case, the Base is $4,000 and the PUA is

$6,000. At any time after Year 1, the minimum amount due is $4,000. However, if the owner has the ability to deposit more than the $4,000 per year up to the full $10,000, the results would be as reflected. If this policyholder did nothing more than what is illustrated here, at age 65 he would have $1,249,756 on which to retire. For most people, that kind of retirement money would be amazing. In addition, his Death Benefit would be $2,372,272. If this person collateralized the entire amount of Net Cash Value at retirement and started taking policy loans—and used the entire Net Cash Value during the rest of his life, the Death Benefit would still pay out in the neighborhood of $1,122,516 to the beneficiary. What other financial instrument can do that? In fact, not seen in this illustration is what would happen beyond age 65. Hint: The compounding doesn't stop but continues to grow until the day of death. I hope you're beginning to see how

		Guaranteed			Non-Guaranteed Assumptions 100% of Current Dividend Scale				
Age	Year	Contract Premium	Net Cash Value	Death Benefit	Contract Premium	Cumulative Premium	Annual Dividend	Increase in Net Cash Value	Net Cash Value	Death Benefit
19	1	10,000	5,826	789,688	10,000	10,000	89	5,914	5,914	789,776
20	2	10,000	11,845	836,268	10,000	20,000	139	6,161	12,075	837,139
21	3	10,000	18,066	881,360	10,000	30,000	189	6,418	18,493	883,392
22	4	10,000	26,414	924,999	10,000	40,000	235	8,597	27,090	928,538
23	5	10,000	36,910	967,224	10,000	50,000	286	10,806	37,896	972,574
24	6	10,000	47,795	1,008,073	10,000	60,000	346	11,264	49,160	1,015,556
25	7	10,000	59,078	1,047,583	10,000	70,000	409	11,739	60,899	1,057,555
26	8	10,000	70,750	1,085,789	10,000	80,000	490	12,224	73,123	1,098,615
27	9	10,000	82,825	1,122,736	10,000	90,000	581	12,737	85,860	1,138,862
28	10	10,000	95,333	1,158,464	10,000	100,000	665	13,277	99,137	1,178,352
29	11	10,000	108,344	1,193,008	10,000	110,000	730	13,873	113,010	1,217,035
30	12	10,000	121,863	1,226,397	10,000	120,000	818	14,499	127,509	1,254,834
31	13	10,000	135,913	1,258,662	10,000	130,000	904	15,152	142,661	1,291,863
32	14	6,996	147,604	1,274,227	6,996	136,996	968	12,898	155,559	1,312,488
33	15	10,000	162,659	1,304,333	10,000	146,996	1,084	16,421	171,980	1,347,878
34	16	10,000	178,279	1,333,406	10,000	156,996	1,207	17,158	189,138	1,382,661
35	17	10,000	194,475	1,361,481	10,000	166,996	1,319	17,903	207,041	1,416,857
36	18	10,000	211,255	1,388,590	10,000	176,996	1,454	18,684	225,724	1,450,441
37	19	10,000	228,628	1,414,764	10,000	186,996	1,600	19,488	245,212	1,483,510
38	20	10,000	246,607	1,440,038	10,000	196,996	1,755	20,324	265,537	1,516,107
39	21	10,000	265,189	1,464,442	10,000	206,996	1,930	21,185	286,722	1,548,281
40	22	10,000	284,397	1,488,009	10,000	216,996	2,109	22,080	308,802	1,580,092
41	23	10,000	304,242	1,510,769	10,000	226,996	2,309	23,016	331,818	1,611,565
42	24	10,000	324,716	1,532,753	10,000	236,996	2,539	23,983	355,801	1,642,779
43	25	10,000	345,807	1,553,990	10,000	246,996	2,785	24,961	380,762	1,673,823
44	26	4,472	362,137	1,555,606	4,472	251,469	3,016	20,557	401,319	1,685,803
45	27	10,000	384,266	1,575,439	10,000	261,469	3,359	26,835	428,154	1,716,585
46	28	10,000	407,000	1,594,614	10,000	271,469	3,711	27,943	456,098	1,747,531
47	29	10,000	430,384	1,613,157	10,000	281,469	4,047	29,086	485,184	1,778,610
48	30	10,000	454,484	1,631,093	10,000	291,469	4,375	30,320	515,504	1,809,745

		Guaranteed				Non-Guaranteed Assumptions 100% of Current Dividend Scale				
Age	Year	Contract Premium	Net Cash Value	Death Benefit	Contract Premium	Cumulative Premium	Annual Dividend	Increase in Net Cash Value	Net Cash Value	Death Benefit
49	31	10,000	479,389	1,648,446	10,000	301,469	4,631	31,590	547,094	1,840,814
50	32	10,000	505,090	1,665,233	10,000	311,469	4,944	32,920	580,014	1,871,698
51	33	10,000	531,557	1,681,474	10,000	321,469	5,301	34,273	614,287	1,902,533
52	34	10,000	558,746	1,697,190	10,000	331,469	5,737	35,671	649,958	1,933,456
53	35	10,000	586,607	1,712,401	10,000	341,469	6,224	37,081	687,040	1,964,627
54	36	9,255	614,404	1,725,300	9,255	350,723	6,781	37,840	724,880	1,994,335
55	37	10,000	643,456	1,739,564	10,000	360,723	7,443	40,027	764,907	2,026,411
56	38	10,000	673,048	1,753,386	10,000	370,723	8,159	41,573	806,480	2,059,190
57	39	10,000	703,188	1,766,787	10,000	380,723	8,885	43,159	849,638	2,092,702
58	40	10,000	733,954	1,779,785	10,000	390,723	9,548	44,796	894,435	2,126,839
59	41	10,000	765,394	1,792,396	10,000	400,723	10,195	46,497	940,932	2,161,448
60	42	10,000	797,469	1,804,637	10,000	410,723	10,918	48,248	989,180	2,196,540
61	43	10,000	830,058	1,816,522	10,000	420,723	11,773	50,006	1,039,186	2,232,288
62	44	10,000	863,046	1,828,068	10,000	430,723	12,753	51,777	1,090,963	2,268,914
63	45	4,333	890,830	1,828,691	4,333	435,057	13,778	47,978	1,138,941	2,295,935
64	46	9,382	923,601	1,838,481	9,382	444,439	14,913	54,507	1,193,448	2,333,523
65	47	9,382	956,614	1,848,009	9,382	453,821	16,048	56,308	1,249,756	2,372,272

this works. In the next chapter you'll learn how to make this even more beneficial throughout your life.

Here's the same illustration, but with the PUA stopped at Year 5. Looking at the Net Cash Value numbers and the Death Benefit on the Non-Guaranteed side (right side) you can see this reduced amount reflected. Again, the reduction is caused by the PUA being removed at Year 5. With a properly structured SDLIC, the owner would still have the ability to continue adding PUA throughout the life of the SDLIC—and he should. Remember, every dollar deposited into the SDLIC will compound for life—uninterrupted. In our everyday lives we deposit dollars into banks. This system should be viewed no differently. Money is stored somewhere, and the SDLIC is the perfect placeholder. Every additional dollar in this system grows both the Net Cash Value and the Death Benefit.

I can't help but make mention of the Increase in Net Cash Value at age 65. That year a deposit of $4,000 is made and the Increase in Net Cash Value is $25,067. That's amazing. Everyone who invests money outside of an SDLIC is hoping for some miracle that can provide similar results. Why go anywhere else—with all the risk—when you can have the most remarkable financial tool working for you day in and

> Nash's Financial-Noise Canceling System <

		Guaranteed			Non-Guaranteed Assumptions 100% of Current Dividend Scale					
Age	Year	Contract Premium	Net Cash Value	Death Benefit	Contract Premium	Cumulative Premium	Annual Dividend	Increase in Net Cash Value	Net Cash Value	Death Benefit
19	1	10,000	5,826	789,688	10,000	10,000	89	5,914	5,914	789,776
20	2	10,000	11,845	836,268	10,000	20,000	139	6,161	12,075	837,139
21	3	10,000	18,066	881,360	10,000	30,000	189	6,418	18,493	883,392
22	4	10,000	26,414	924,999	10,000	40,000	235	8,597	27,090	928,538
23	5	4,000	31,080	924,999	4,000	44,000	241	4,930	32,020	930,303
24	6	4,000	35,936	924,999	4,000	48,000	252	5,139	37,159	932,058
25	7	4,000	40,982	924,999	4,000	52,000	264	5,351	42,511	933,835
26	8	4,000	46,206	924,999	4,000	56,000	283	5,559	48,070	935,640
27	9	4,000	51,611	924,999	4,000	60,000	305	5,774	53,844	937,517
28	10	4,000	57,216	924,999	4,000	64,000	322	6,003	59,847	939,467
29	11	4,000	63,072	924,999	4,000	68,000	328	6,276	66,123	941,443
30	12	4,000	69,179	924,999	4,000	72,000	358	6,570	72,693	943,416
31	13	4,000	75,540	924,999	4,000	76,000	382	6,867	79,560	945,486
32	14	4,000	82,180	924,999	4,000	80,000	411	7,193	86,752	947,624
33	15	4,000	89,073	924,999	4,000	84,000	460	7,515	94,267	949,866
34	16	4,000	96,234	924,999	4,000	88,000	511	7,857	102,124	952,288
35	17	4,000	103,665	924,999	4,000	92,000	553	8,195	110,319	954,874
36	18	4,000	111,361	924,999	4,000	96,000	613	8,547	118,865	957,594
37	19	4,000	119,333	924,999	4,000	100,000	676	8,915	127,780	960,501
38	20	4,000	127,576	924,999	4,000	104,000	746	9,291	137,071	963,599
39	21	4,000	136,090	924,999	4,000	108,000	822	9,673	146,743	966,903
40	22	4,000	144,883	924,999	4,000	112,000	899	10,069	156,813	970,414
41	23	4,000	153,963	924,999	4,000	116,000	986	10,487	167,300	974,127
42	24	4,000	163,315	924,999	4,000	120,000	1,087	10,907	178,207	978,071
43	25	4,000	172,936	924,999	4,000	124,000	1,191	11,331	189,539	982,267
44	26	4,000	182,811	924,999	4,000	128,000	1,314	11,766	201,304	986,723
45	27	4,000	192,946	924,999	4,000	132,000	1,472	12,242	213,546	991,502
46	28	4,000	203,334	924,999	4,000	136,000	1,636	12,726	226,273	996,670
47	29	4,000	214,000	924,999	4,000	140,000	1,787	13,228	239,500	1,002,201
48	30	4,000	224,982	924,999	4,000	144,000	1,929	13,770	253,271	1,008,025
49	31	4,000	236,333	924,999	4,000	148,000	2,043	14,346	267,616	1,014,075
50	32	4,000	248,037	924,999	4,000	152,000	2,177	14,932	282,549	1,020,290
51	33	4,000	260,081	924,999	4,000	156,000	2,333	15,532	298,080	1,026,716
52	34	4,000	272,433	924,999	4,000	160,000	2,526	16,139	314,219	1,033,411
53	35	4,000	285,064	924,999	4,000	164,000	2,743	16,747	330,966	1,040,441
54	36	4,000	297,965	924,999	4,000	168,000	2,992	17,384	348,350	1,047,853
55	37	4,000	311,081	924,999	4,000	172,000	3,287	18,014	366,364	1,055,715
56	38	4,000	324,396	924,999	4,000	176,000	3,603	18,658	385,022	1,064,086
57	39	4,000	337,919	924,999	4,000	180,000	3,922	19,324	404,345	1,072,966
58	40	4,000	351,694	924,999	4,000	184,000	4,207	20,014	424,359	1,082,289
59	41	4,000	365,740	924,999	4,000	188,000	4,483	20,731	445,090	1,091,972
60	42	4,000	380,046	924,999	4,000	192,000	4,791	21,471	466,561	1,102,009
61	43	4,000	394,540	924,999	4,000	196,000	5,161	22,202	488,764	1,112,475
62	44	4,000	409,155	924,999	4,000	200,000	5,582	22,916	511,680	1,123,460
63	45	4,000	423,838	924,999	4,000	204,000	6,051	23,621	535,301	1,135,035
64	46	4,000	438,569	924,999	4,000	208,000	6,538	24,334	559,635	1,147,232
65	47	4,000	453,362	924,999	4,000	212,000	7,024	25,067	584,702	1,160,031

day out with almost no risk? It would be crazy not to!

Here's a bonus. If you follow the IBC system, guess how much tax will be paid on the Increase in Net Cash Value or the Death Benefit when it pays out? The answer is *none . . .* ever! In case you missed that—nada, zip, zero! Intrigued? It's true. It's also another reason why I'm passionate about sharing this concept!

Chapter 6

Banking with the SDLIC

Because the SDLIC has a special ability to emulate a bank, I want to turn our attention to the Net Cash Value column of our sample illustrations in the previous chapter. The contract owner has full authority to access almost 100 percent of these amounts. Owners of Specially Designed Life Insurance Contracts are earning more money on their deposits, without being subjected to undue risk, creating personal interest earnings and dividends. With ever-increasing Net Cash Value, as an SDLIC owner, you would have your own banking cash machine, so to speak. You could utilize this Net Cash Value in an infinite number of ways 24/7/365.

R. Nelson Nash's book *Becoming Your Own Banker* gives great examples of how to use your money as an Infinite Banker. I highly recommend reading that book to gain additional understanding of the banking concept using an SDLIC. As a contract owner, the basis of the concept is to borrow the available cash value and repay yourself with interest. Nash explains additional strategies to invest within an existing SDLIC. It supercharges an already high performance financial engine, which increases both the cash value and the death benefit.

Let's say you have a sum of accumulated money from your job and your savings. All funds in an SDLIC are using after-tax dollars, meaning income was earned and taxes were paid on said money. Before owning an SDLIC, typically you would have put your money in some kind of investment or in a bank for distribution. When using these systems, once you spend money it's gone; and you can't earn any further money from it. Your money has been exchanged for goods or services, and that's that.

On the other hand, if you make a deposit into an SDLIC while retaining your bank account, you can move money from the SDLIC to your bank for direct cash purchases. However, the money you move from the SDLIC to the bank does not actually deplete your SDLIC by the amount you move in the same way it would if you moved it from a bank or a 401(k) or an IRA. The available Net Cash Value is collateralized against the Death Benefit of the SDLIC, and the actual funds come from the insurance company's own separate pool of money. All insurance companies have this system, but only a small number of companies let policyowners borrow money from the pool. From my research, this SDLIC borrowing and repayment strategy is unknown to most insurance agents. The ease with which this money can flow between the insurance company and the SDLIC owner is for the most part unknown in the insurance industry.

The insurance company's pool of available cash is used for paying out death benefits and investing. All types of insurance companies have this pool of money. Most companies are not equipped to move the money in and out of their systems for the purposes of the IBC.

I'm confident that people would not use banks to finance their purchases if they knew about SDLICs. As Infinite Bankers, people can use their SDLICs for major and minor purchases that are usually made with credit cards. These credit card purchases are controlled by—and benefit—a bank. However, making said purchases within the SDLIC will benefit one's own estate. You could think of a bank as a foreign institution because the bank—rather than you—controls the value and price of your financial decisions. As you will understand by continuing your study and reading Nash's book, paying interest to your own personal "bank," which is housed in your SDLIC, would be significantly more financially favorable for you, as opposed to paying interest to a foreign institution such as your local bank.

Imagine the scenario in which you take your money (bypassing the bank) and place it into an SDLIC. Then you borrow from the available cash value of the contract to buy a $20,000 car. In doing this, you aren't only *thinking* like a bank, you're *acting* like a bank. You would plan a repayment schedule to your SDLIC for the car loan. In addition to the principal repayments, you could pay more than the minimum principal payment and/or a higher interest than the market rate because—if you're thinking like a bank—the higher the principal repayments and/or interest, the more quickly you'll repay yourself. Think of it as making more than the required minimum payment to yourself, which accelerates the repayment of the loan.

At the end of the repayment schedule, set by your own made-up amortization schedule, you'll own the auto *and* you will have repaid the loan to your SDLIC. Just as a bank would charge interest, you *charge* and *pay yourself* interest. By doing so, you will increase the value of your SDLIC on multiple fronts. Once you've paid yourself back, your SDLIC's full cash value will be back where it was (plus interest) before you took the car loan; and your internal banking system will have even more available cash value to utilize. Again, behind the scenes, the SDLIC compounds all your premium payments, interest earned, and dividends throughout the life of the contract—in other words, for the rest of the owner's life. The same money is creating value for you in four places: the interest you pay yourself on the car loan, the continually compounded monies within the SDLIC, the ever-increasing death benefit, and the enjoyment of ownership of your new car! Use this system in any number of ways to finance your family's life.

One would probably assume that we must pay taxes on all income we earn, whether it's wages or investment income.

But this system is different. The SDLIC system predates our Internal Revenue tax code. An SDLIC owner could use the money in the contract any time prior to the death benefit payment by either withdrawing up to the full available cash value or borrowing up to the full available cash value at any time. The IRS will tax a withdrawal, but *it will not tax borrowed money*. As an Infinite Banker, one would only borrow and *never* withdraw.

Banking within your SDLIC offers substantial flexibility. SDLIC owners can choose their own repayment schedules—or make the choice not to repay loans to their contracts at all. (Legally, the insurance company will get the borrowed money back when the death benefit is paid out by subtracting the borrowed cash from the death benefit as stated earlier.) This gives the owner options in the event of any personal life crisis, such as an accident or unexpected medical expenses. Additionally, the loan amounts may be used in the owner's golden years for living expenses. Remember, however, unlike a 401(k) or IRA, the principal, interest, and dividend continue to compound on all monies ever deposited into the system. So, even when money is borrowed, more money is created in the system, including the death benefit. Where else can that happen? Actually . . . nowhere.

SDLIC owners should repay the loans on their own repayment schedules—and with interest. Not mentioned earlier, as of this writing, life insurance companies charge about five percent simple interest on the outstanding loan balance on an annual basis, for loans taken from an SDLIC. Traditionally, any institution you would normally use for lending would charge you interest. It matters not the percent, because you'll always overcome it by paying your SDLIC back the five percent (in this case). This additional interest will go to the SDLIC's bottom line, accelerating your loan repayment.

Keep in mind . . . money that isn't growing is stagnant. Think of a stagnant pool of water compared to a fresh running stream. I'd rather drink from a running source instead of a stagnant pool. The same vitality process works with money. Keep it moving, keep it growing through uninterrupted compounding of principal, interest, and dividends. Why isn't everyone utilizing this concept? Simply because it's unknown to the masses. Steve Jobs said it best, as stated earlier. If we only would have known . . . but now we do!

After you spend money from a traditional bank account, that money is gone. A person can't make further use of it because it's a one-way action. It's also called an *opportunity cost*, meaning that whenever you spend, save, or invest your money, it costs you the opportunity to use that money elsewhere. People relinquish control of their money by passing it into the hands of financial institutions' programs like IRAs and 401(k)s. Losing control of your money means losing your ability make money on your money.

Again, consider the example of buying a car. Typically you would pay cash, get a loan, or lease it. If you bought the car with a loan, you would own it; but the bank would get the principal and the interest. Utilizing the IBC system, at the end of the day you would still own the car . . . and retain the principal and interest too. Win, win, win!

I want to be clear that the IBC is not the same as a bank. The IBC system designs a financial vehicle that mimics certain banking functions in your private economy, giving you "infinite" possibilities of using and reusing your own money. It's like a bank—but better! It allows you to take command of your financial future in a realistic and powerful manner.

However, using your money over and over again through the Infinite Banking process gives you never-ending internal and external returns on your money, with reduced or even no market volatility. At the end of your life, you can take great satisfaction from creating ongoing returns for your family legacy. That is priceless!

Chapter 7

Critical Thinking

The First Paradigm Shift

As we begin our descent for landing, or rather our time together here, I'd like to share a thought before you go any farther in the book. The following represents a lot of the reasons why most of us have been in a financial system that's hard to understand, hard to navigate, and ultimately concludes with a very questionable outcome.

"If you do not know what the problem is,
you won't know how to fix it."

This was one of the first revelations R. Nelson Nash shared with me. It was the first critically challenging thought he gave me. He let me dwell on it for some time before moving forward with the Infinite Banking Concept. I realize the Infinite Banking Concept is still new to you and likely counter to everything you've ever learned about money.

I challenge you, just as Nash challenged everyone, to think critically about the process of fixing your finances, and see it for what it is and what it has to offer. I've used that sentence of Nash's a lot in my life; I'd like to challenge you to think critically about how it can be applied to yours.

So, what are you looking for in your financial world? Does what you've read so far help with that question?

If I could sum up this book in one sentence, here's how it would read:

If you had a financial vehicle that you owned 100 percent, that continued to grow with a guarantee, compounding every cent of principal, interest, and dividends for life, tax free—along with full liquidity as needed, no matter what—and an insured death benefit at the end of life for your heirs, how much money would you want to put into it—a little, or a lot?

Most of us have grown up seeing the world as a place of limitation rather than a place of inexhaustible rewards. In reality, the financial world treats you more or less the way you expect to be treated, just like everyone else does. Understanding what you're looking for and the problem you're facing is your new beginning to true financial success—or any kind of success, for that matter.

Years ago, after college, my first real job landed me working for a major defense contractor. It wasn't a flying job, yet it was working in the aviation and engineering field. I happened to be working on a project that was labeled as "classified." This meant that I couldn't share information about what I did with anyone outside the project confines.

I was about a year into the job. One night after work, I went home to my apartment and, as usual, sat down and turned on the TV to relax and catch up on the events of the day. With no internet back then, it was typical for me to watch the news.

The local Dallas/Fort Worth news broadcast began discussing the project I just happened to be working on. *The project!* The coverage sounded so real, just as if it were all first-hand knowledge. They were even showing pictures of buildings where I worked.

The conversation went on for several minutes—about a classified project. I was awestruck. When the segment ended, I thought to myself, *What did I just see?!* For 99.9 percent of the people watching it, they would have believed everything as described in the report.

It goes without saying that most people who know little or nothing about a specific topic all tend to want to believe what's being shared or stated, right? It's hard to disagree when you know so little about something. Most don't take the time to gain further knowledge because, well, it takes time, something that most people lack.

For those of us actually working on the specific project in the news segment, we already knew that almost none of what had been reported was true. My thoughts raced. *How could the media have made up the entire story and played it on the news?* It was such a turning point in my young adult life. Up to this point, I had trusted the news for accurate information. But there it was, my first real piece of seen-and-understood disinformation. It was my first mental paradigm shift.

I thought, *If they just made up that story, what then, should I understand to be true about the rest of the information that comes from the news, media, or anything else, for that matter?*

I began to wonder how much of what I had watched in the past had been misleading. I've come to this conclusion about much of the information of which I have little or no direct knowledge: it's suspect at best. With that in mind, looking farther back in time, my formal education never prepared me for real world financial understanding. How about you?

The older I get, the more clearly I see. And you? As I stated in the beginning of the book, when we were at David's house years ago, listening to him explain the IBC system, it was just another incredible moment of clarity about how the financial system actually works.

Consider and relive everything you've been taught about money. After getting this far in the book, have you learned anything contrary to what you had previously understood about money and investing? I hope so. This question keeps running around in my mind almost daily: *What is bigger, the amount of knowledge I know, or the amount of knowledge I don't know?*

It's been said that the average person reads only one book after high school. How can that be? Think of all the books that have ever been written. There are so many different topics, it just boggles the mind. It's all that knowledge, just waiting to be shared. I want more knowledge, and I believe you do too—or you'd be doing something other than reading this book.

I wrote the book to help you on many levels. I realize you'd probably never heard of IBC. I get that. I hadn't either. If you're like me and so many others, finishing your first IBC book is just the beginning of your IBC journey.

Considering all the other types of available investment options, it's not hard to imagine the difficulty—and time—it takes to understand it all. There are so many alternatives, but they all have that one thing in common: risk—with mostly unknown outcomes.

You've been taught for years to accept financial risk because, well, it's normal; but it's not normal to take risks. In most cases, we try to avoid risk-taking like flying a plane, parachuting, trying a different hair style, driving super-fast, maybe talking to or meeting people we don't know, or trying a new and exotic food. You get the picture. But the same isn't true with the money system as we know it. Risk is an expected, and even encouraged, part of how the Wall Street system operates.

Acquiring wealth from Wall Street is said to be a fairly complex process. "Trust your Wall Street adviser," they say. However, every adviser seems to recommend a different risky strategy. How come? It's because no one person has the simple solution to acquiring wealth.

They have many different strategies of risking your money and then waiting to see what happens. In most cases, it takes a lifetime to see the results. Factor in any kind of market volatility, social security reform, inflation, Medicare reform, and taxes, and you'll quickly see that the math just doesn't add up. It's a scary consideration. Their system is based on fear and greed.

The rules of the game of money, as you know, are mostly Wall Street and government rules. Most people don't have the discipline or patience to follow the rules. They want to get rich quick instead of getting rich slowly—and for sure.

Consider, for example, the fact that those invested in the stock market or housing market will want to sell at some point, right? Did you ever think that you might not be able to sell because you might not be able to find a buyer as a result of market circumstances? It could happen. Liquidity doesn't always happen in their system. And that's a big deal.

Your life, your family's life, your retirement, and your estate planning all hinge on what you do *today* for tomorrow and the years ahead. This is something to strongly consider; however, most people don't.

What you do today matters. The days and years ahead will come much sooner than you think. Just pull out your phone and start looking at pictures from last year, or worse, five years ago. Where has the time gone?

Do you want to guess and wait, taking a chance to see what your money might look like in the future? Or would you like to see clearly what it *will* look like? *Understanding the problem matters.* Time matters. Risk matters. Clarity matters. Truth matters. The solution matters. This is all about you and the generations that will follow you.

The Bamboo Tree and the Yield Curve

By now, you have a basic understanding of the IBC SDLIC system. It's *the tool* to build a *bulletproof financial foundation* from which to create the rest of your financial world and future. Your strong financial foundation will support your strong financial building. The remainder of this chapter will touch on several areas of interest that are the most discussed topics in my practice.

The SDLIC, much like a bamboo tree, takes several years to grow its foundation or root system. When the bamboo tree finally breaks the surface of the ground after several years, it is amazing to see its rate of growth. The same thing happens with the SDLIC.

The number one question most people ask is . . . "Why haven't I heard about this before?" The answer is simple—*and obvious, once revealed:* The Wall Street system is rigged! But why?

The government and Wall Street system forces you to take 100 percent of the risk, *with your money,* guaranteeing only one thing: *a completely unknown outcome.* It's true.

Yet their system administrators (the companies between you and the product you're buying) have a 100 percent chance of making money because we use *their* rules while they use *our* money! Most people haven't considered this, but I'm guessing you have by now, because you're this far into reading this book. The mainstream system loves the *sheeple*—you know, the non-thinking people!

Those mainstream companies charge fees in good and bad economies. They use our money—and risk it—to make their money every day. Whether or not we make money doesn't matter to them like it matters to us. *They always get paid.* If they didn't get paid, they wouldn't be in business. I see their advertisements boasting "No Fees." Are you kidding me? If they didn't collect a fee somewhere in the system, well, they couldn't exist. Now, I'm not anti-capitalism. In fact, I love capitalism. What I am against is the financial smoke and mirrors and all the regulations that hinder success.

At this point, you might be wondering how an IBC practitioner earns a commission. Regarding the commission associated with the SDLIC, the insurance company has incorporated it into the illustrated spreadsheet presented in Chapter 5. Every illustration and its projected spreadsheet reflect all ongoing principal premium deposits, interest gains, and dividend gains, which include its servicing fee. It's all in black and white. There are no "additional" fees.

Wall Street would never teach a system like the Infinite Banking Concept. And why is that? Simple: *It doesn't let them use our money.* If they don't use our money, they can't make money. IBC is the last system they'd ever want anyone to discover. But, as I said earlier in this book, they do use the IBC-type products in their COLI and BOLI products. It's good enough for them, so why not us?

Again, Wall Street and the government push financial products like ETFs, other types of funds, derivatives, IRAs, 401(k)s, 529 college savings plans, and custody services. If I were to ask you to explain what an ETF or mutual fund was, could you? Could you explain the differences between them?

Within these products, bankers and brokerages can charge ongoing transaction, management, and custody fees for their services. It's the lifeblood of the Wall Street bankers' profit-making gambling machine.

On the other hand, the IBC system can be the dawn of your new financial life and the solution to your financial problems. It has the real possibility for changing your family's financial legacy . . . for generations. It has true dynasty implications for your family.

Now, I understand this is probably your first real understanding of our financial system—our money system. I was in your shoes; and I assure you, the more you study this system, the more clarity you'll gain. What is it you're looking for? R. Nelson Nash always used to say, "If you know what's really happening, you'll know what to do! Rethink your thinking!"

The Infinite Banking Concept allows your money to benefit all areas of your life—with 100 percent control. You can finance your life's ongoing needs, your savings, your retirement, and your estate planning (a.k.a. independence) with 100 percent unlimited access to all your available cash value. Now, that's liquidity! Plus, you'll have a yield curve that never inverts—along with a zero tax liability . . . for life!

Now wait a moment—have you ever heard of the term *yield curve*? Even if you haven't, I'll bet you've seen one—you just didn't know its name. A yield curve is the graph used to represent a gain and/or loss over time. In this case, let's consider the stock market, real estate, or any other typical investment.

At any given moment, there are gains and losses within industries. Over a period of time, you can simply connect the gains and losses to create a yield curve. The typical yield curve moves up and down and up and down over time, kind of like a jet when it's in the air.

Consider this question: When is it a good time to buy or sell, to add or subtract to any mainstream investment? The only reasonable answer to the question? It depends. If you need instant money, it would be a time to consider removing it for use somewhere else—but only if that's possible. Outside market conditions will dictate liquidity. Even if you could liquidate, the investment would stop working for you immediately upon liquidation.

On the other hand, if you have extra money available, it may be a time to consider making a deposit into an investment vehicle, but the outcome of that investment would always be in question—except in the SDLIC. Now, let's further consider the SDLIC and its yield curve. It's not complicated. In fact, it goes only one direction. Up! From the moment you start your own SDLIC, your yield curve can do nothing but increase.

As stated earlier, just as the cash value increases each year, so does the uninterrupted compounding of principal, interest, and dividends. Once the SDLIC is established, you are covered both in the near term and the long term. After all these years, that fact excites me just as much today as it did when I first learned about the Infinite Banking Concept.

Sound Money, Unsound Money, and Inflation

You will remember we discussed fiat money previously, right? Check back in Chapter 3 to refresh your memory. To further that discussion, let's dig deeper to clarify its meaning with these financial terms: *sound money (non-fiat) versus unsound money (fiat)*, and *inflation*.

Sound money just sounds good, doesn't it? *Sound* means that the money is supported—or backed—by something. As was stated earlier in the book, in the United States, this was money that was once supported by gold!

On the other hand, *unsound money* is backed by . . . nothing. Actually, it has been told to us that it's the good faith of our government that backs our money. Words versus gold. Which one would you rather trust to back your money?

The US dollar is truly unsound (fiat). All the countries in the world now have fiat money. It's only as good as the governments that back it up. In many countries, the money situation doesn't look good at all. As mentioned in the chapters before, our US dollars are ever increasing in number, both in paper currency and fractional reserve banking.

As our dollars continue to be produced on demand both by the government through the central banks and via fractional reserve banking, the dollar's value keeps decreasing—and it always will. Further, the government wants to keep increasing the money supply; thus the government wants to *keep* inflation.

Do you remember August 15, 1971, when we experienced a huge *financial* earthquake? It was the day President Nixon separated the US dollar from the gold standard monetary system. It was a big deal; however, most people did not understand the consequences of this action.

Immediately, the dollar had no foundational basis for actual value.

At that time, one ounce of gold equaled $38 US dollars. Once the split happened, our government began creating more new dollars and increasing the money supply. This single action began a cascading financial landslide for the people of our great country. With this new fiat money crept in one of the most silent killers of our monetary system and family estates.

Inflation. It's *the* financial thief. It steals our money every day, every year. It's a silent and hidden erosion of value for *every* dollar ever created. We have no control over it. The exact amount of inflation currently eroding our dollar is variable, an ever-changing number. Inflation kills savings potential. Spendable fiat is more valuable today than tomorrow. However, the SDLIC gives you flexibility without eroding its ever-increasing growth.

Let's examine an instance of a current inflation projection model. *If* the rate of inflation stays as it is today, the cost of a similarly valued home past, present, and future will look like this over time:

> In 1915 a typical house retailed for $4,500.
> In 1965: $45,000
> In 2015: $450,000
> In 2065: $4,500,000
> In 2115: $45,000,000
> *(This is less than 100 years from now.)*

Shocked? I was—and I still am. If for no other reason to consider the SDLIC, this should push you into having further conversation with us at The Financial Prodigy. We encourage you to learn how the IBC SDLIC system might work for you and your family. *Your age doesn't matter.* Remember that.

You're preparing the future for yourself and/or your family. It may happen the way you plan, or it may not. Are you going to leave it to chance? What does the *opportunity* cost of your money and time look like between now and the end of your life?

Do you recall what the term *opportunity cost* means?

It has to do with the financing of your life and how your money is working (or is not working) for you at all times. As explained earlier, after you spend money from a traditional bank account, that money is gone. A person can't make further use of it because it's a one-way action. It's also called an *opportunity cost*, meaning that whenever you spend, save, or invest your money, it costs you the opportunity to use that money elsewhere.

Remember, the available cash value inside the SDLIC can be used now and until death without any restrictions. In fact, it can be used in and throughout future generations if set up correctly in your estate planning.

Think about your kids. The opportunity cost of them needing money for a car, their education, or a home can be covered by the SDLIC. However, if you're using the bankers' and government system, in most cases, these things can't be accomplished without losing a lot of your money through interest and taxes. Besides, you'd be missing out on the uninterrupted compounding of IBC dollars.

By the continued process of inflation, our government confiscates, secretly and unobserved, a tremendous part of our wealth. This process engages all the hidden forces of economic law on the side of destruction and does it in a manner which not one man in a million is able to diagnose.

Now, consider this: The difference in value between one ounce of gold and the unsound fiat has dramatically increased. Today, one ounce of gold is equal to about $1,600 dollars—and it's ever increasing. This clearly shows that the buying power of the dollar has eroded significantly.

By all accounts, the current price of gold is severely understated. It's being artificially suppressed by the system overseeing our fiat. I believe the true value of gold to be much higher than is currently represented. I say this because the amount of money created in the last fifty years has proportionally not matched the small increase in gold prices.

The way the sound monetary system used to work prior to 1971 and the way our government had to function back then is unimaginable today. They had to be fiscally responsible. They couldn't just keep creating new dollars. They had to operate as we should in our lives today. The federal government doesn't need to live within its means because it owns the money machine.

Today, our government and the central banks can increase the money supply almost at will to continue paying off the creation of unsound-dollar interest (debt interest), increased budgets deficits, and the like. Doesn't that seem improper? Taxes are not how this government funds itself. It's the continued creation of fiat money. What we do with this unsound money matters even more today than it ever has.

There is some good news within this conversation as it relates to sound versus unsound money. From our perspective, there are two kinds of dollars within the IBC system: the IBC dollar and the non-IBC dollar.

The IBC SDLIC "dollar" is very different from every other saved or invested non-IBC dollar. Why? Because whatever you do with your non-IBC dollars outside of the IBC system puts into question its further benefit, if any.

Whenever you deposit dollars into the IBC SDLIC, those dollars will *never* stop working to benefit you—not ever! The IBC SDLIC dollars keep gaining uninterrupted compounding of principal, interest, and dividends, along with the family security of the included death benefit. Again, the yield curve continues its positive upward climb *for life*. As you're thinking about this, you can clearly understand how the IBC SDLIC dollar performance plays out. Remember, borrowing IBC dollars from the SDLIC does not affect the yield curve or the death benefit. When using the borrowed IBC dollars outside of the SDLIC, you can rest assured that the IBC dollars in the SDLIC are still performing as illustrated; and that makes a huge difference compared to every other type of non-IBC dollar savings or investment.

The yield curve never inverts—never goes negative—*if* properly operated within the IBC SDLIC system, which is a very important point. It's the certified IBC practitioner who's the only pilot qualified to bring your IBC financial flight to a successful landing.

It works because we're not *removing* the IBC-dollars from the SDLIC specifically; rather we're *borrowing* against the stated cash value from the insurance company. *Its system is truly genius.* You never have to be concerned about market timing to use the available cash value. Use it anytime without risk of losing the uninterrupted compounding and an ever-increasing yield curve.

Saving versus Investing

The general population has blurred the line between the words *saving* and *investing*. The two have seemingly become one. Since the beginning of the 401(k) and the IRA, most people have confused the two terms. But they're not the same. Not even close.

Saving is what people used to do with their money. (Remember checking and savings accounts?) We used to make deposits into banks because of their perceived safety in storing our dollars for future use. You could "know" for sure that you always had access to your money when you needed it—and it was gaining some value with the interest you were paid. Banks, in the past, enticed us to save our money with them by paying a reasonable interest rate.

Unknowingly, some people today are still depositing money in these savings-type accounts and certificates of deposit (CDs)—but at significant losses. "How is that?" you ask? Think about inflation. Think about opportunity cost.

Currently, the rate of inflation is *officially* running in the

2–3 percent range. Who really knows what its actual number is? If the saving accounts or CDs are paying out anything less than the 2–3 percent range—and they are—the depositor is losing money.

Many times the CD locks up the individual's money for *years*. If you needed to finance your life during the locked window of time, you'd have to borrow money and pay interest to, say, a bank. More lost money. Then, of course, there is the tax on the paltry gain.

Can you see how the system is set up for us to lose value and take a loss? Think of the hamster wheel. People keep running to get ahead; but, in reality, they're just getting more tired and making no headway. Good news—the SDLIC will beat the inflation factor and save the opportunity cost.

For most people, the incentive to save money in traditional savings vehicles has decreased substantially. Over the last few decades, the central banks have been reducing the prime interest rate to very low numbers, taking away the incentive to save. In fact, below I'll be discussing "negative" interest rates. Buckle up!

Originally, investing—as opposed to saving—was to be used with excess dollars and was looked at as a way of increasing our monies *outside* the perceived safety of banks. Basically, it's legally gambling our money in the hope of making significant gains and winning in the Wall Street *gambling* stock market, housing market, or other financial opportunities. Today, *savings* and *investment* are essentially considered to be the same thing. But in reality, that's not the case. One has risk, but the other doesn't. They both have significant opportunity cost.

Consider the NASCAR fan. Now, whether you're a fan or not, I'd like to pose a question: Do most people sit through the entire race to see who wins at the last possible second? I personally don't believe that's the primary consideration. No, we watch the race . . . to see the crashes. Even as gruesome as that sounds, why else would anyone sit for hours and hours to watch cars go 'round and 'round and 'round? That seems so boring—at least to me.

I tend to believe that most people are doing that very same thing in just about every financial services sector. Everyone's waiting and watching for the next crash. It's a constant concern. Of course, in the financial sense, most people are trying to *avoid* the inevitable crash. If timed just right, by some miracle, it's possible to avoid the financial crash. But how can you tell when that might happen? The word *possible* is something to consider strongly, but rarely does anyone get it right. Thus, we have recessions and depressions.

I believe a reason for the 2018–2019 rise in the US market is the ongoing creation of fiat money and its use by corporations for the purpose of financing its own stock buybacks (at very attractive rates of interest). This stock buyback or stock repurchase looks attractive to the Wall Street market. Why? Because it *appears* to the outside world that there's an increase in demand for the specific stock, which, in turn, increases its perceived value. It keeps the stock value artificially elevated. This isn't the only reason for this rise—but it is a part of it (certainly a conversation for another day). The buybacks cannot go on without corrections. I believe when the market curtails its amazing climb, the fallout will negatively impact countless families. The situation is kind of like when a jet runs low on fuel; it's going down, just as the market will. How far and when, nobody knows.

In every other kind of investment, it's all about the random chance of getting the timing right and avoiding the crash. Why worry when you have the best financial foundation underneath your financial house? You know by now what I'm referencing: the Infinite Banking Concept's SDLIC solution.

I constantly hear radio ads soliciting interested parties to attend a seminar and learn how to buy and sell equities (stocks, mutual funds, and the rest). The same thing goes for real estate. They say, "Learn how to reduce your risk by studying this system of picking stocks" . . . or buying real estate . . . or something else. Or, "Learn why risk is 'normal' and should be accepted as part of your investment strategy." Again, it comes down to risk tolerance and timing. Unless you're a very motivated person willing to spend many hours studying the system and babysitting the investment, the odds of success are heavily slanted against you.

Think about this: Less than 20 percent of the "professional" traders on Wall Street outperform the S&P 500. Do you remember what the S&P 500 is? We mentioned it back in Chapter 1. It's a stock market index that measures the stock performance of 500 large companies listed on stock exchanges in the USA. A stock market index is a measurement of a section of the stock market. It's computed from the prices of selected stocks.

What are the odds that you'll pick one of the professionals within the 20 percent who actually offer a chance of winning in the stock market—or any other market? Further, what are the odds that you beat one of those professional 20 percent with only the information you acquire from a financial seminar or from just being out there all by yourself reading charts and news reports? At the time of this writing, March 2020, the stock market crashed over one thousand points per day—for three days straight. What the market future holds is always in question. This market reaction was in response to a virus that started in China and has the possibility *if not probability* to infect much of the world's population. What could be the next issue to cause a market correction—today or anytime in the future? I see this as a financial black hole.

Compare this to a professional pilot. It takes years of training before a pilot can successfully fly a commercial jet. Even then, pilots don't start out as captains. They spend years learning more from the airline captains before upgrading to the captain position themselves.

The bigger question is this: Would you like only 20 percent of captains to have successful flights? How about the odds of having a seat on one of the 20 percent of successful flights? You see, there's no place for risk in aviation. And this brings up another important question: How much risk should we have in our financial world? It takes a lifetime to see the results of investing in the current markets. Most people unknowingly fly blindfolded with their financial outcomes in question. Waiting until the end of your working years—while blindfolded—is not a good strategy for a successful flight or for your profitable retirement and succession plan.

By now you should recognize how the SDLIC is a foundational "savings" tool that can be used as a way to utilize its ever-increasing available cash value to further "invest" as well. With the SDLIC, you get both.

The IBC dollars can be used in an infinite number of ways once you get started. Yes, you can even use the IBC dollars to buy stocks, mutual funds, real estate, automobiles, and even a Cryptocurrency like Bitcoin. You can use those IBC dollars to pay for college—and your next vacation too.

Actuarial Science

Have you ever heard of the term *actuarial science*? It represents the very refined mathematical equations that create the IBC SDLIC. Actuarial science is the driving force behind the SDLIC's yield curve. The mathematical formula of actuarial science is based on millions of lives, both in the past and into the future. It can reveal the odds of just about any outcome.

In our case, the actuary looks at several areas of interest. The biggie is the life expectancy of the SDLIC policyholder. (Actuarial science can predict this timeline with amazing accuracy.) Based on one's health and age, along with several other factors, the actuaries can project the individual's life expectancy and the required financial values they must have available at any given date to accommodate each SDLIC's financial obligations. The illustrations reveal the SDLIC's future projections. No other investment can do this.

The mutually owned company can know with a high degree of accuracy what their financial needs will be to remain profitable today, as well as decades into the future. This knowledge gives the SDLIC the financial foundation, growth, and death-benefit guarantees that make it such a special and unique product. When you compare actuarial science mathematics to the guessing game in all other financial instruments, it's hands down a no-brainer.

Negative Interest Rates

Are you familiar with the term *negative interest rate*? As of early 2020, Japan and a number of countries in Europe are experiencing negative interest rates that have been put in place by some governments and world central banks. And more, negative interest rates are slowly spreading around the globe. Worse yet? If more countries through the central banking system move in that direction, our country won't escape this expanding policy. Why? Because the US fiat currency valuation would be out of balance with the rest of the world's fiat currency.

To clarify, if the US fiat dollar paid more interest for savings, all other world fiat currency would buy US fiat to increase their money supply. More money, more spending ability. This would give the US dollar more buying power around the world. Goods and services around the world would be cheaper for us, and more expensive for the rest of the world. That would give us an imbalance in trade. That would—and does—create trade issues.

Here's how part of negative interest rates work—and how they may affect you and me. Instead of banks paying interest to customers for their deposits, banks charge users to deposit money in their institutions. Yup. Imagine that. So, what will this do?

First, people will opt to put their money elsewhere. But where? We won't want to deposit money in a bank and pay for the privilege of doing so. Who wants to pay the banks more money to store their dollars? (Remember: We already do that with the fees they charge.)

Negative rates of interest will force the general population into either spending all monies or "investing" in some kind of risk-based system. It will be the way our government, through the central bankers, will keep us buying more consumer products than we need, or using their financial products like the 401(k).

Storing money in any system currently paying interest or having an annual rate of return (gain) of 3 percent or less is slowly losing money without your even knowing it because the current inflation rate is at least 2–3 percent per year, even before taxes are applied.

And there's another *hoped-for* result of negative interest rates: The central bankers desire a steady state of increased inflation. There it is again—inflation rearing its ugly head. You can't even bury your money in your yard because inflation will eat away at it. It's a lose-lose situation.

The central banks also want to avoid deflation (an increase in the value of the fiat dollar). Does that make sense to you? Deflation is something that the banking sector dislikes. Deflation causes the dollar to have more buying power. As I've stated here and in previous chapters, inflation causes the dollar to decrease in value. *Inflation is a huge silent tax.* There's no way to escape inflation in our current fiat money system. The government prints; inflation results.

Quick sidenote: When the US and other countries were financially connected on the gold standard with sound money, governments had a limited amount of spendable money. They were on a fixed income, so to speak. They could create more money, but they needed to mine or own more gold to do so. This means the government could actually run out of available money. When all the countries around the world had limited money, each was limited with spending on things like war, infrastructure, and growth. Interesting, right? Can you see what unsound money has done? It's mind boggling.

But what about the future? The IBC SDLIC is a great solution to negative interest rates. As discussed above, a number of other countries are already experiencing negative rates and its effects. Again, it's a consequence of unsound money. This is a bigger discussion than the confines of this book; but for now, you're seeing the problem for what it is.

The Business Owner/CEO
Are you a business owner or CEO? In addition to your personal life, as a business owner, consider these little-known or little-used sections of the IRS tax code—sections to benefit you, your business, and its employees. The following sections are beyond most businesses' IRS-scripted business plans like the 401(k) and can be incorporated into the IBC product with no IRS oversight. The IRS Section 162 Executive Bonus Plan and the Nonqualified Deferred Compensation plans (NQDCs) Section 409A and 412(e)(3) are amazingly beneficial once you understand how to incorporate them with IBC. The plans offer tons of flexibility and options for the business and employee without the headache, oversight, and attention that the IRS-qualified plans mandate.

The mandates of the well-established Wall Street, central bank, and government financial systems are tied together, forming a monopoly with the US fiat dollar and the American people. Their mandates make us take all the risk, locking our money up for years, then make us finance our life in another part of their system, thus paying them interest. All the while they make money on every cent of our money all day long, every day, with no real risk to them. When you think about it, they want your money locked up in their system for as long as they can, applying well-placed penalties should you choose otherwise. Why would they want to change their system? They wouldn't. It benefits them—and not us.

The Infinite Banking Concept is a way to *secede from their system*. By reading this book, you've begun to have a clearer vision of the way the world's money system really works. Just as a pilot has to learn how to use the navigational instruments to fly in the clouds and have a successful flight, we need to have clarity about how the money system works. When you have the proper knowledge and training, you can critically think through different systems and outcomes. You, too, can be a part of the IBC movement away from their system and toward a new system that benefits you, your family, and your business—and not someone else!

We all need a financial tool to overcome these and other financial issues.

Think Risk versus No Risk.
Think Taxes versus No Taxes.
Think No Control versus Control.
Think Non-Liquidity versus Liquidity.
Think Unsound money versus Sound Money.
Think Negative Interest Rates versus IBC.
Think Ever-Growing Yield Curve.

This is about . . . *thinking differently.*

Every day matters—no matter what your age!

The Infinite Banking Concept is your foundational financial solution.

Chapter 8

The Most-Asked Questions

Why haven't I heard of the Infinite Banking Concept before?

The answer is simple.

Wall Street and the government systems force you to risk 100 percent of your money, guaranteeing only one thing: a completely unknown outcome.

It's true.

Yet, their system administrators have a 100 percent chance of making money because we use their rules while they use our money!

They charge us fees in good- and bad-performing economies. They use and risk our money to make their money every day.

It doesn't matter. They always get paid.

Wall Street pushes financial products like ETFs, other fund types, derivatives, and custody services. Bankers and brokerages can then charge transaction, management, and custody fees on them . . . It's the lifeblood of the Wall Street Bankers' profit machine.

They would never teach a system like the Infinite Banking Concept. It does not let them use our money. If they don't have access to our money, their money machine stops.

Their system is akin to riding a roller coaster with your money. A New York Times article, published February 9, 2011, referred to the Infinite Banking Concept this way: "It's viewed as an insider's secret for the affluent: a legal way to invest . . . all without paying taxes on the gains."[1]

This is the dawn of your new financial life. It has the real possibility for changing your family's financial legacy . . . for generations.

The Infinite Banking Concept allows your money to benefit all areas of your life, with 100 percent control.

You can . . . finance your life's ongoing needs, your savings, your retirement, and your estate planning, all with 100 percent access to your money when needed, a yield curve that never inverts, and a zero tax liability—for life!

You don't need a financial degree to grasp the concept nor to implement the simple system. Someone once said, "Like a parachute, the mind works best when it is open."

This is the financial answer you've been looking for, always wanted, but just never knew it existed.

Robert Kiyosaki once said, "The rich don't do things differently than the poor, they do the exact opposite."

Why does IBC come across as ideologically biased?

I realize the conversation in this book discusses the Infinite Banking Concept as the first major step in building your financial house. It's certainly not the only piece of your financial building.

There are many building "add-ons" that can be included in your entire financial portfolio. The emphasis is on the IBC as your foundational platform. Having this system in place, including all its attributes, makes it a no-brainer foundational asset.

In reality, building upon the SDLIC is not mandatory, but then you would be seriously shortchanging yourself and your family. Using its available cash value to finance your life significantly decreases your chances of lost opportunity cost and the addition of what would otherwise have been lost interest to outside sources.

The time value of money is absolutely essential if you are to efficiently use and grow your wealth. With the SDLIC, your financial world opens up a whole new opportunity for your financial growth. Can you imagine your money working for you in at least two different places at once—for the rest of your life? It's a big example of the power your money can provide.

The concept of time value of money can be described like this: Typically, we'd rather use our money now, not later. For example, if you can use $10,000 now or in five years, you'd choose to use it now, all other things being equal. This is because the ability to spend the money immediately, an almost certain benefit, is superior to the uncertainty of spending it in five years, especially considering the inflation effect.

Similarly, if you invested the $10,000 or put it in a bank savings account earning interest (or paying interest due to negative interest rates) during these same five years, then you'd have to wait for the ability to use whatever the gain or loss was at a future date. Seen through the lens of IBC, time-related opportunity cost is the reason that the concept of time value of money is key in managing both personal and business finances.

The Infinite Banking Concept gives you both the utilization now and the enjoyment of its uninterrupted growth that continues for life. To the best of my knowledge, the SDLIC is the only financial tool that allows this concept to flourish.

How does the SDLIC yield curve work?

As discussed briefly in Chapter 7, the yield curve brings a significant benefit to the IBC SDLIC. With respect to only the SDLIC, the yield curve shows the value of how uninterrupted compounding of all monies inside the SDLIC works. I know of no other investment that enjoys a yield curve that never ever inverts. In the SDLIC, the yield curve always climbs in a positive direction. That statement is huge. Even better, the special attributes of the SDLIC's ability to lend money from itself and still never lose the continued, uninterrupted compounding of all its monies . . . is miraculous. Review the following two yield curve graphs. Which one works best for you?

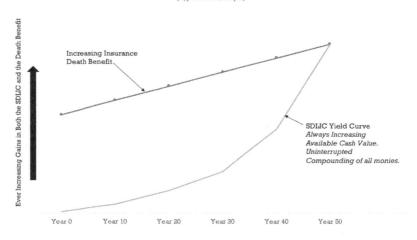

IBC SDLIC
Never Inverting Yield Curve
(Hypothetical Example)

Ever Increasing Gains in Both the SDLIC and the Death Benefit

Increasing Insurance Death Benefit

SDLIC Yield Curve
*Always Increasing
Available Cash Value.
Uninterrupted
Compounding of all monies.*

Year 0   Year 10   Year 20   Year 30   Year 40   Year 50

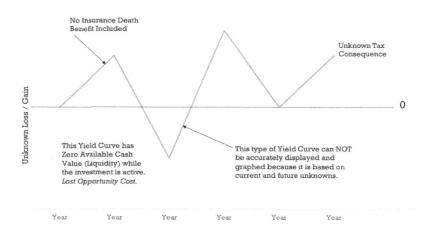

Typical Financial
Inverting Yield Curve
(Hypothetical Example)

No Insurance Death Benefit Included

Unknown Tax Consequence

Unknown Loss / Gain

0

This Yield Curve has Zero Available Cash Value (Liquidity) while the investment is active. *Lost Opportunity Cost.*

This type of Yield Curve can NOT be accurately displayed and graphed because it is based on current and future unknowns.

Year   Year   Year   Year   Year   Year

Is there any downside to owning an SDLIC?

The only answer I typically give is this: The biggest down-side is that your parents didn't know about the IBC when you were born. The fact that you've read this far indicates that you have a willingness to know more. I suggest reaching out to our office to further discuss any concerns you may have. Time matters; delaying the conversation can impact you for life. Best of all, it's free to have the conversation.

How am I going to fund my IBC SDLIC?

Suffice it to say, you'll need to begin thinking differently about how your money will be working for you. The SDLIC is the tool to construct your foundation, upon which you'll build the rest of your financial future.

You'll always spend, save, or invest your money some-where, right? When you fully grasp the Infinite Banking Concept, you'll understand the significance of running as much of your money through the SDLIC system as possible.

You use a bank today, and you have no problem deposit-ing money into it. The IBC is utilized in a similar manner. It's a system that unfolds over time. Utilizing a portion of your current monies is all that is needed. The key is simply adjust-ing where you put it before it's spent or stored.

You don't need to create additional money to start an SDLIC; rather you'll use existing funds to build it. This isn't blindly done without a financial game plan. As an IBC autho-rized practitioner, I can share ideas for your specific situation so you can develop a plan to fund your SDLIC.

If you're like most people, you're giving up a lot of money paying interest on debt. As referenced earlier, capturing that outgoing debt is of high importance if you're going to get ahead. Where you direct your outflow of money should be where you start when considering an SDLIC.

With regard to using 401(k) and/or IRA monies, that is a topic for you to discuss with your CPA or tax advisor. They

113

probably won't understand the IBC, but they will understand withdrawing monies from these government-qualified plans and how that will impact you. It certainly can be utilized in creating an SDLIC, but only after you have a clear understanding from your CPA or tax advisor about the tax consequences. Everyone has a pool of money. It's typically stored in several places. Wherever the money comes from, it can be used to start an SDLIC.

I have a Roth IRA, I've already paid the taxes, and my investment is tax free. How can IBC help me?

You've paid taxes upfront on your Roth IRA. However, you still have unnecessary risk in the stock market, you don't have access to your money—maybe for years, and politicians could change tax policies at any time on the Roth or standard IRA, or even the 401(k). In addition, you don't have a death benefit that pays out multiples on the cash value.

On the other hand, if your money was invested instead in an SDLIC, it's typically as easy as making an emailed request for access to all the available cash value 24/7/365. This simply doesn't happen in the IRA world. When you're using your own money and not someone else's to finance your life, your financial world will change beyond what you ever imagined.

Teresa Ghilarducci, professor of economics at the New School for Social Research, published a brilliant article in the New York Times, "Our Ridiculous Approach to Retirement." She bundled all the investment challenges we face into the following:

Not yet convinced that failure is baked into the voluntary, self-directed, commercially run retirement plans system? Consider what would have to happen for it to work for you. First, figure out when you and your spouse will be laid off or be too sick to work. Second, figure out when you will die. Third, understand that you need to save 7 percent of every dollar you earn. (Didn't start doing that when you were 25 and you are 55 now? Just save 30 percent of every dollar.) Fourth, earn at least 3 percent above inflation on your investments, every year. (Easy. Just find the best funds for the lowest price and have them optimally allocated.) Fifth, do not withdraw any funds when you lose your job, have a health problem, get divorced, buy a house or send a kid to college. Sixth, time your retirement account withdrawals so the last cent is spent the day you die.[2]

So the secret about the Roth IRA and 401(k) plans is this: You don't need to have one to build a retirement. No one in their right mind should start one, and if you have one, you should reassess why—and consider the SDLIC as the alternative.

The sponsors of 401(k) plans are being fined, penalized, or forced to make reimbursements for the plan errors. The average fine is $600,000. Fidelity, one of the largest 401(k) sponsors, settled two class-action lawsuits for $12 million . . . after being sued by its own employee over excessive fees.

You mentioned that the insurance company charges simple interest when a loan is taken from the SDLIC. How does that work?

Yes, that's true. In brief, within the SDLIC, there are two kinds of interest addressed. Simple and compounded. Simple interest is paid to the company annually on the outstanding balance of any loan against the SDLIC. Simple interest is tabulated on only the outstanding loan balance—and once a year.

For example, if one dollar from the available cash value of the SDLIC was taken as loan, and the insurance company was paid five percent upon the anniversary of the loaned dollar, the borrower would owe the sum total of five cents. In recent years, and as of this printing, about five percent has been the going rate for simple interest.

Unlike most other types of loans, as the principal loaned amount decreases over time, the amount of the interest paid to the insurance company decreases. That's because the principal amount of the loan is less, which translates into less interest paid to the insurance company. The outstanding simple interest is always prorated down as the principal is reduced.

I'm a business owner; how can this be applied in my business?

There are many favorable ways the SDLIC can be utilized within a business. Let's start by asking where you store the money that you set aside for your impending taxes. You pay either quarterly or less frequently. Currently, that money is stored somewhere. A bank? Why not in an SDLIC?

Consider this: once that same money is held in the SDLIC, you will forever reap uninterrupted compounding on every cent in the system, even though you eventually pay Uncle Sam out of the SDLIC. Remember, you can request the money anytime and redeposit it anytime too. Think banking system, storage system for your money.

Ever want to add equipment or grow the business? Many times business owners borrow the money from a bank. Why not start a system where you could borrow from yourself? R. Nelson Nash has a great explanation of equipment financing in his book *Becoming Your Own Banker*.

As a sidenote, if the major investment banks in this country have more than $400 billion stored in life insurance called BOLI (bank-owned life insurance), it seems logical that it would be useful to the rest of us business owners too, right?

Consider IRS Section 162. This section of the IRS code is little used, but it has great benefits for the business owner. For example, an employer can add additional compensation to the employee, both through the cash value and the life insurance inside the SDLIC.

Within this funding, the employer can design future payouts in several different ways. It could take place as a bonus payment plan, as in a Key Man insurance policy. The role of Key Man insurance is to protect the company in the case of a key person's death or loss of employment. A key person represents someone who is critical to the business operation. The loss of this person would create a significant hardship on the company operation.

Another option is called a golden handcuff policy. This is used to retain a valued employee, creating an incentive to remain with the company for a set number of years, as agreed to within a separate contract. In fact, both Key Man and golden handcuff policies can be used concurrently if needed.

These are but a few ideas, each being free from IRS oversight as non-qualified compensation plans, which are unlike most other qualified plans. In fact, the employer has the ability to share unequal amounts of bonus-type funds to employees through Section 162. This section gives the employer a lot of flexibility with employee compensation and is far less complex than the standard qualified plans the IRS oversees. Again, I would refer you to your CPA or qualified tax professional to discuss the various options.

Is an insurance company a safe place for my money?

Insurance companies are among the safest places for your money. Consider billionaire business magnate and philanthropist Warren Buffet. He made much of his wealth in his insurance businesses. The life insurance companies that IBC Practitioners use rank among the best of the best, and they are among the safest of all financial institutions.

As noted earlier, the Comdex ranking system is used by the financial industry. Comdex is a composite index based on the rankings that companies have earned from the leading rating services, including A.M. Best, Standard & Poor's, Moody's, Fitch Ratings, and TheStreet.com. One can compare the Comdex rankings of insurance companies, on a scale of 1 to 100, to find the best companies.

Corporations call their corporate-owned life insurance COLI. Here's a sample list of companies that own COLI of the more than 700 Fortune 1000 companies. Time Warner, Johnson & Johnson, Harley-Davidson, Verizon, Disney, GE, and Walmart.

Should you desire to investigate the amount of bank-owned life insurance (BOLI) a bank has, navigate your browser to fdic.gov. As of the writing of this book, these are the instructions for conducting a search: At the top of the page, place your cursor over "Industry Analysis," then click on "Bank Data & Statistics." Select "Institution Directory," and select "BankFind" at the top right. Simply enter the institution's name and click on the search button at the bottom of the page. It will bring up certificate numbers of the biggest banks within the institution you named. Click on "Generate History." Around pages 35–45 (varies with institution), you can find the life insurance assets section, which lists the cash value life insurance assets that the institution owns. As shown at the beginning of the book, the banking world has more than $400 billion invested into COLI alone.

Digital Journal issued a press release October 6, 2017, titled "Why 401(k) Founder Regrets 'Monster' He Helped Create; Financial Investigator Pamela Yellen Reveals Where 401(k) Founder Ted Benna Now Puts His Money." It reads, in part,

> Early supporters of the 401(k) now warn consumers against participating in the revolution they started. Two-time New York Times bestselling author Pamela Yellen investigated the savings strategy now advocated by the founder of the 401(k) and has some surprising findings.
>
> Ted Benna is credited with being the "father of the 401(k)," for finding a way to capitalize on the tax code to create a way for working men and women to

supplement the pension plans many workers used to have. Those pensions plans have been disappearing, and 401(k)s were created to help pick up the slack. But over the years, Benna watched Wall Street and Big Business pervert the 401(k) in ways he couldn't possibly predict. For at least six years he has been calling the 401(k) a "monster" that "should be blown up."

Benna recently announced that he's put a substantial part of his own money—"probably the biggest part of my wealth"—into another kind of savings plan. What is he using? Pamela researched the question to discover Benna has put most of his money into high cash value, dividend-paying whole life insurance, commonly known as Bank On Yourself type plans—the alternative savings strategy she has advocated for years.

Pamela can discuss the history of the 401(k) and how government and companies used it to replace guaranteed pensions with risky stock investments to the peril of Americans everywhere.

"Wall Street has been extremely successful at getting us to buy into 401(k)s, IRAs and similar government-sponsored retirement accounts lock, stock and barrel," she says. "Most people have little or no savings outside of these vehicles, according to the Federal Reserve Survey of Consumer Finances. But the chorus of experts warning of the dangers of 401(k)s and IRAs keeps growing."[3]

It sounds too good to be true! Is it?

Once I may have agreed, but the numbers don't lie. Those who start handling their money as infinite bankers are thrilled when they see the growth and value this system generates over time. It's a real and viable option—or better yet, financial solution!

119

Major banks have more than $400 billion worth of whole life insurance in their executive compensation plans. Large corporations have executive compensation plans with whole life insurance, including SDLICs. Politicians and the rich have been using this IRS-sanctioned approach for decades. Why not the rest of us? Because they use our money in their system, making us take all the risk.

The typical government-sponsored retirement accounts handcuff the user in so many ways. On top of that, they can't tell you what the value of your 401(k) or IRA, stock, mutual fund, or real estate will look like tomorrow, much less 20, 30, 40 years from now. They keep using people's hard-earned money, charging fees both ways, along with the occasional scandals—with no real shot at accurately predicting outcomes.

The IBC through the SDLIC builds the most solid financial foundation possible. From this foundation you can erect your financial building, which will withstand the effects of the world's financial storms.

As I've stated before, the SDLIC is the only asset in existence that offers uninterrupted compounding of principal, interest, and dividend growth—free from income, dividend, and capital gains tax. All this is wrapped in the best Tier 1 financial savings asset. Again, in the financial world, a Tier 1 asset is the safest place to store money.

How does an insurance company make money to pay interest and dividends?

Insurance companies have successfully done actuarial studies for more than two centuries to accurately forecast and price risk. These companies sell a variety of life insurance products that produce income. They use the float strategy, in which money is temporarily held and then invested conservatively. These insurance companies have investment income generated from government bonds and commercial real estate, along with a wide variety of conservative investments—all of which create cash and interest income. They have public financial statements that can be viewed openly.

Is this a one-and-done system?

Great question! The answer is simple. It depends on what your goal is. Let me ask you a question: If you were a bank owner and your bank was doing so well that you were looking for a place to put your excess money to work for you, what would you do? If you say, "I'd open another branch office," I'd say you understand the IBC. Congratulations! The power of this concept, once understood and implemented, could not only change the destiny of your family, it's truly multi-generational and could pay for generations. If only our parents had possessed this knowledge, think of the head start we would have had!

I'm ready to learn more. How do I find an Authorized Practitioner?

Actually you already have. Please contact me, S. Paul Horsley, at our office by simply emailing your request to:

sph@thefinancialprodigy.com
or scheduling an appointment here:
ScheduleMyWebinarNow.com

We'll be happy to help you continue learning and further your understanding of the IBC and how it can work in your life. We can assist you in procuring your own IBC policy or policies and coach you in how to best utilize the system.

---

[1] "Tax-Free Life Insurance: An Untapped Investment for the Affluent," Lynnley Browning, The New York Times, accessed April 24, 2018, https://archive.nytimes.com/www.nytimes.com/2011/02/10/business/10PRIVATE.html.

[2] "Our Ridiculous Approach to Retirement," Teresa Ghilarducci, The New York Times, Accessed April 4, 2018, https://www.nytimes .com/2012/07/22/opinion/sunday/our-ridiculous-approach-to -retirement.html.

[3] "Why 401(k) Founder Regrets 'Monster' He Helped Create; Financial Investigator Pamela Yellen Reveals Where 401(k) Founder Ted Benna Now Puts His Money," Digital Journal, Accessed April 4, 2018, http:// www.24-7pressrelease.com/press-release/why-401k-founder-regrets -monster-he-helped-create-444834.php.

Chapter 9

The Conclusion

Thank you for taking the time to educate yourself on *Why the Rich Don't Die Broke*. You now understand more about the fiat money system than 99.9 percent of the US population. Having taken the time to educate yourself separates you from almost all other citizens of our country. That is huge—congratulations!

If you have enjoyed reading this book, we hope you'll share it with others you care about. Most people will never have the opportunity without the help of people like you.

It is now time for you to consider your next step. If you are considering moving forward to learn more about the subject, I encourage you to reach out to our office. There is no cost to have the conversation that could very well change your family's financial future.

Below I've listed a summary of points that can keep you focused on many of the benefits of the Infinite Banking Concept.

- Use your current household monies to begin enjoying the use of uninterrupted compounding of principal, interest, and dividends 24/7/365 for your entire life.

- Reuse your money over and over, without losing any of the internal compounding of principal, interest, or dividends.

- Form a yield curve that never inverts, that stays positive and ever growing for life.

- Shield your money from the risks and losses in the stock market and other financial institutions.

- Shield your money from taxation on your gains inside the system.
- Predict growth for your money.
- Begin to capture all current and future interest you pay on debts from all sources.
- Gain 100 percent access to your money with no hidden fees or penalties inside the system.
- Overcome inflation and deflation.
- Legally pass money on to your heirs tax free.
- Create a multi-generational financial fortress while using your own money in an ongoing, as-needed basis.
- Rely on a system with a track record dating back more than 200 years.
- Create a rock-solid financial foundation from which everything else grows.

In 2020 the stock market hit an all-time high. How high will it go? Will it continue to rise, stay where it is, or decrease—and how rapidly? Real estate is at an all-time high. The same financial "monsters," specifically subprime mortgages and collateralized debt obligations (CDOs), that crashed the housing market in 2008 are rearing their ugly heads again with a different name: the "bespoke tranche opportunity" (BTO).

According to an article in *US News & World Report*, BTO is investment-industry lingo that could be translated as an investment that's custom tailored (bespoke) by the investor, and is a piece (tranche) of the private securities market. But it could be taken as another CDO-like "investor maze with a shiny new 'For Sale' *sign*."[1]

Today, the auto industry has the same subprime loan issues as the housing sector of 2008. The interest rates that banks are paying on savings and certificates of deposit (CDs) are a fraction of a percent above nothing. Because of that, the rate of savings in the USA is at its lowest point in decades. We're taxed on more than half of every dollar we earn, from the moment it comes to us until the moment we use it. Debt in this country is at an all-time high in mortgages, credit cards, auto loans, and student loans.

When does the next 2008 happen? That's like asking when the next terrorist attack will happen. What effect will any of this have on our personal and national economies? Are you ready for it? It may not come tomorrow, or next week, but it will come. The time to protect yourself and your family is *now*.

As of this edition (2.0), there has been a tremendous amount of volatility within the stock market and the oil markets around the world. The values within the US stock market have been rapidly declining over a very short period of time. Many people are concerned about their savings and retirement, as well they should be.

Time horizons are so important when considering what to do with your savings. Are you assured that your money has a chance to work for you without significant risk or loss? This book is about the one system that I have faith in to overcome it all: The Infinite Banking Concept using a Specially Designed Life Insurance Contract, through a mutually owned, dividend-paying whole life insurance company.

This is the secret of *Why the Rich Don't Die Broke: The Financial Prodigy's Secret of the Wealthy*. This is how you can substantially improve your family's financial story. You can set yourself free from traditional banking, 401(k)s, IRAs, 529 college savings plans, qualified government sponsored programs, and the crazy Wall Street casino. Nothing else gives you the same flexibility and freedom while continuing to pay out uninterrupted compound principal, interest, and dividends for life like the IBC system does.

It is my hope that this book has done its job to inform you about what I believe is the best way to invest your money.

As an Infinite Banker, you can mimic the banking process to grow your wealth with minimal risk and build a foundation of financial security for your family for generations. The Infinite Banking Concept stands far above the wide array of other savings and potential investment strategies. It gives you a valuable tool to generate an internal return through uninterrupted compounding of principal, interest and dividends. At the same time, Infinite Banking gives you the ability to reap an external return by investing the same cash value in multiple ways to meet your life's needs.

If you'd like to learn more about IBC and talk to a Certified Infinite Banking Practitioner, please contact us at sph@thefinancialprodigy.com or visit our website, www.thefinancialprodigy.com.

You may order R. Nelson Nash's book, *Becoming Your Own Banker: Unlock the Infinite Banking Concept* from Amazon.com. This book is another foundational study in the understanding of the Infinite Banking Concept, and it's written in straightforward terms. You need not be a financial wizard to enjoy it and benefit from it!

"The Infinite Banking Concept is not a bank; it's a thought process that represents a major paradigm shift."

—R. Nelson Nash

[1]"Ghost of 'The Big Short' Haunts Wall Street; Bespoke tranche opportunity resembles the financial instruments that wrecked the housing market," Lou Carlozo, *US News & World Report*, Accessed April 4, 2018, https://money.usnews.com/investing/articles/2016-05-23/what-is-a-bespoke-tranche-opportunity.

Now that you have a basic understanding about the Infinite Banking Concept, if you're like most people you're wondering what the next step should be. I congratulate you for taking the first step in your understanding of IBC. That is HUGE!

You probably also have questions about how to start an IBC system of your own. That's *normal*! Every day that goes by without an SDLIC is one less day of compounding. I would recommend that you give me a call or send me an email. Everything starts with your taking the next step.

To inquire about how to begin the process of starting your own IBC system, please contact us here:

S.Paul Horsley
sph@thefinancialprodigy.net
(715) 210-5517
To schedule an IBC Zoom webinar, go here:
Schedulemywebinarnow.com

Infinite Banking Concepts®
Authorized Practitioner

A good man leaveth an inheritance to his children's children.
— Proverbs 13:22

Thank you for taking the time to read this book!

Recommended Reading

(arranged in order of importance)

The Holy Bible, God

Becoming Your Own Banker: Unlock the Infinite Banking Concept, R. Nelson Nash (Infinite Banking Concepts, 2009 4th edition)

Building Your Warehouse of Wealth, R. Nelson Nash (Infinite Banking Concepts, 2012)

Financial Independence in the 21st Century, Dwayne Burnell and Suzanne Burnell (Financial Ballgame Publishing, 2012)

A Path to Financial Peace of Mind, Dwayne Burnell (Financial Ballgame Publishing, 2010)

Retirement Heist: How Companies Plunder and Profit from the Nest Eggs of American Workers, Ellen E. Schultz (Portfolio, 2011)

The 7 Deadly Innocent Frauds of Economic Policy, Warren Mosler (Valance Co Inc, 2010)

Fed Up: An Insider's Take on Why the Federal Reserve is Bad for America, Danielle DiMartino Booth (Portfolio, 2017)

The Pension Idea, Paul L. Poirot (Foundation for Economic Education, 1950)

Economics in One Lesson, Henry Hazlitt (Crown Business, 1988)

Zero Hour: Turn the Greatest Political and Financial Upheaval in Modern History to Your Advantage, Harry S. Dent, Jr. (Portfolio, 2017)

The Creature from Jekyll Island: A Second Look at the Federal Reserve, G. Edward Griffin (American Media, 2010)

Thou Shall Prosper—Ten Commandments for Making Money, Rabbi Daniel Lapin (Wiley, 2009)

Unfair Advantage: The Power of Financial Education, Robert T. Kiyosaki (Plata Publishing, 2011)

Made in the USA
Las Vegas, NV
11 February 2025

17883919R00075